A GUIDE TO CRIMINAL LAW

Peter Robertson

Emerald Publishing
www.straightforwardco.co.uk

Emerald Publishing
Brighton BN2 4EG

ISBN 1903909 98 8

Printed by Webspeedbooks Bedfordshire
www.webspeedbooks.com

Cover design by Straightforward Graphics

Whilst every effort has been made to ensure that the information
contained within this book is correct at the time of going to
press, the author and publisher can take no responsibility for the
errors or omissions contained within.

Contents

Introduction

Table of cases

3.   Unlawful Killing   49

Table of cases

Adamoko 1995 AC 171
AG v Whelan 1934 IR 518
Arioboke 1998 Crim LR 314
Bainbridge 1960 1 QB 129
Beckford 1988 AC 130
Briggs 2003 EWCA Crim 3662
Caldwell and Lawrence 1982 AC 341
Calhaem 1985 QB 808
Camplin 1978 AC 705
Chamberlaine v Lindon 1998 1 WLR
Chan-Fook 1994 1 WLR 689
Church 1966 1 QB 59
Collins 1973 QB 100
Collins and Wilcock 1984 1 WLR
Coney 1883 8 QBD 534
Cunningham 1957 2 QB 396
Cunliffe v Goodman 1950 2 KB 237
Duffy 1949 1 ALL ER 932
Dytham 1939 QB 722
Goodfellow 1986 83 Cr App R 23
Hale 1978 68 Cr App R 415
Hardie 1985 1 WLR 64
Hill v Baxter 1958 1 QB 277
H L Bolton (Engineering) Co Ltd v T J Graham and Sons
Ltd 1957 1 QB 159
Invicta Plastics Ltd v Clare 1976 RTR 251
Ireland 1998 AC 147
Instan 1893 1 QB 450
Jaggard v Dickinson 1981 QB 527
Johnson 1989 1 WLR 740
Johnson v Youden and Others 1950 1 RB 544
Jones 1990 1 WLR 1057

Lamb 1967 2 QB 981
Larkin 1943 KB 174
Latimer 1886 17 QBD 359
Leach 1969 The Times 15th January
London Borough of Harrow v Shah and Shah 2000 Crim LR 962
Martin 1881 8 QBD 54
Miller 1954 2 QB 282
Mitchell 1983 QB 741
MPC v Charles 1977 AC 177
Mousell Ltd v London and North Western Railways Ltd 1917 2 KB 836
National Coal Board v Gamble 1959 1 QB 11
Pagett 1983 76 CR App R 279
Pearson 1992 Crim LR 193
Pitham and Hehl 1977 65 Cr App R 45
Pitwood 1902 19 TLR 37
Prince 1875 LR 2 CCR 154
Rance v Mid-Downs Health Authority 1991 1 QB 587
Re A (Children) 2000 EWCA Civ 254
Re London and Globe Finance Corporation 1903 1 CH 728
Robinson 1977 Crim LR 173
Samuels v Stubbs 1972 4 SASR 200
Scott v Shepherd 1983 2 Wm BI 892
Sofroniou 2003 EWCA 3681
Smith v Chief Superintendent of Woking Police Station 1983 76 Crim App R234 Crim LR 323
Smith 1974 QB 354
Smith and Morgan 2000 UKHL 49 AC 146
Steer 1988 AC 111
Stevens v Gurley 1859 7 CB NS 99
Sweet v Parsley 1970 AC 132
Thomas 1985 81 CR App R 331
Tuck v Robson 1970 1 WLR 741

Wacker 2003 EWCA Crim 1944 4 AlL ER 295
Wilcox v Jeffrey 1951 1 ALL ER 464
Williams 1992 1 WLR 380 2 ALL ER 183
Williams (Gladstone) 1987 3 ALL ER 411 78 Cr App R 276
Willer 1986 83 CR App R 225
Wilson 1955 1 WLR 493
Woollin 1998 UKHL 28
Woolmington v DPP 1935 AC 462

Introduction

This latest book in the *Emerald Home Lawyer Series* is a companion volume to Emerald Guide to The English Legal System.

This guide is comprehensive and in-depth and aims to introduce the reader, whether student or layperson, to criminal law as it affects our daily lives.

The book commences with the development of law generally, as to understand the context within which criminal law operates, it is first necessary to understand the workings of the legal system.

Following this, the purpose of criminal law is outlined, along with an examination of areas of criminal law, such as unlawful killing, specifically murder and manslaughter. The area of non-fatal offences against the person is examined along with property offences and obtaining property by deception.

The areas of criminal damage and defences generally in criminal cases are outlined along with inchoate offences. Finally, the book looks at the legal system and how it operates on a day-to-day basis when hearing criminal cases.

Overall, this introduction to criminal law is wide ranging and is illustrated throughout with relevant cases. The book will prove invaluable either as a student handbook or as a guide for the professional or layperson who wishes to enhance their knowledge of criminal law.

1

The Development of Law

The law in England and Wales has developed gradually over time. Law has been developed in a number of different ways, and the methods of developing law are known as sources of law. Historically, the most important ways were custom and decisions of judges. Parliament became more powerful in the eighteenth and nineteenth centuries, with Acts of Parliament becoming the main source of new laws, although judicial decisions were, and are, still important. During the twentieth century, statute law and judicial decisions continued to be the main sources of law, but increasingly two new sources of law became important: delegated legislation and European legislation. Together, all these sources of law have combined to create the present day legal system. We shall be looking further at sources of law in the next chapter, the purpose of criminal law.

Customs

Customs are rules of behaviour which develop in a community. There are two main types of custom: general and local customs.

General customs

General customs are common customs that have developed and have been absorbed over time into law.

Local customs

Local customs is a term used where a person claims that he or she is entitled to some local right, such as a right of way or the right to use land in a certain way, because this is what has happened locally over time. Judges have a test of what constitutes local customs. These are as follows:

- The custom must have existed since 'time immemorial
- The custom must have been exercised peaceably openly and as of right
- The custom must be definite as to locality, nature and scope
- The custom must be reasonable

It is very rare for a new custom to be considered by courts nowadays. There have been certain exceptions. For example, in Egerton v Harding (1974) the court decided that there was a customary duty to fence land against cattle straying from the common. Although customs develop they are not part of the law until recognised by the courts.

Common law

The legal system historically could not rely on customs alone. In Anglo-Saxon times there were local courts that decided disputes but it was not until after the Norman conquest in 1066 that a more organised system of courts developed. Norman kings realised that control of the country was that much easier if the legal system was also controlled. William the Conqueror set up the Curia Regis (The Kings Court) and appointed judges to hear disputes from the nobles. In addition to this central court, judges were sent to major towns to decide important cases.

In the time of Henry 11 (1154-89) these tours became more regular and the country was divided up into circuits, or areas for the judges to visit. Initially the judges would use the local customs or the old Anglo-Saxon laws to decide cases. On return to London the judges would discuss customs and gradually these evolved into a uniform or common law.

Common law is the basis of our law today, an unwritten law that developed from customs and judicial decisions. The phrase 'common law' is still used to distinguish laws that have been developed by judicial decisions, from laws that have been created by statute or other legislation. For example murder is a common law crime whilst theft is a statutory crime.

Common law also has another meaning. It is used to distinguish between rules that were developed by the common law courts (the Kings Courts) and the rules of equity which were developed by the Lord Chancellor and the Chancery Courts.

Equity

Historically this is an important source still playing a part today with many of our legal concepts having developed from equitable principles. The word 'equity' has a meaning of fairness and this is the basis on which it operates.

Equity developed because of problems in the common law. Only certain types of cases were recognised. The law was also very technical; if there was an error in the formalities the person making the claim would lose the case. People who could not obtain justice in the common law courts appealed to the King. Most of these cases were referred to the Kings Chancellor. This was because the Chancellor based his decisions on principles of natural justice and fairness, making a decision on what seemed right in a particular case as opposed to the strict following of previous precedents. Account was also taken of what the parties had originally intended.

To ensure that decisions were fair, new procedures were introduced such as subpoenas, which ordered a witness to attend court. New remedies for compensation were developed which were able to compensate plaintiffs more fully than those previously used. The main equitable remedies were: injunctions; specific performance; rescission and rectification. These are all still in use today and will be explained more fully later on in this book.

Judicial precedents

The doctrine of precedents

Judicial precedent refers to the source of law where decisions of judges in the past create law for future judges to follow. This source of law is also known as case law and is a major source of law.

The English system of precedent is based on the Latin maxim *stare decisis et non quieta movere* Whish is usually shortened to *stare decisis* and which translated means 'stand by what has been decided and do not unsettle the established'. This supports the idea of fairness and certainty in law.

Ratio Decidendi

Precedent is only relevant and can only be effective if the reasons for past decisions are known. Judges will outline reasons for decisions and the rationale for a judgement outlining the principles of law used. These principles are an important part of any judgement and are known as the *ratio decidendi* which means the reason for deciding. This is what creates the precedent for future judges to follow.

Obiter Dicta
The remainder of the judgement is called *obiter dicta* (other things said) and judges in future cases do not have to follow it.

Original precedent

If the point of law in a case has never been decided before, then whatever the judge decides will form a new precedent for future cases to follow. As there are no past cases for a judge to base his decision on, he is likely to look at cases which are the closest in principle and he may decide to use similar rules. This way of arriving at a judgement is called reasoning by analogy. The idea of creating new law by analogy can be seen in Hunter and others v Canary Wharf Limited and London Docklands Development Corporation (1995). Part of the decision involved whether the interference with television reception was capable of constituting an actionable private nuisance. The facts of the case were that the main tower Canary Wharf built in the Isle of Dogs East London, was 250 metres high and 50 metres square. The claimant and others claimed damages from the defendant for continuing interference over a number of years with the television reception in the area as a result of the height of the tower.

In the Court of Appeal, the Lord Justice Pill stated:

'Lord Irving (counsel for the defendants) submits that interference with television reception by reason of the presence of a building is properly to be regarded as analogous to loss of aspect (view). To obstruct the receipt of television signals by the erection of a building between the point of receipt and the source is not in law a nuisance............... I accept the importance of television in the lives of people. However, in my judgement the erection or presence of a building in the line of

sight between a television transmitter and other properties is not actionable as an interference with the use and enjoyment of land. The analogy with loss of prospect is compelling. The loss of a view, which may be of the greatest importance to householders, is not actionable and neither is the mere presence of a building in the site lines to the television transmitter'.

Binding precedent

This is a precedent from an earlier case which must be followed even if the judge in the later case does not agree with the principle. A binding precedent is only created where the facts of the second case are sufficiently similar to the original case.

Persuasive precedent

This is a precedent that is not binding on the court but the judge may consider it and decide that it is a correct principle and is persuaded that it should be followed. Persuasive precedent comes from a number of sources:

- Courts lower in the hierarchy
- Decisions by the Judicial Committee of the Privy Council
- Statements made obiter dicta
- A dissenting judgement
- Decisions of courts in foreign countries.

The hierarchy of courts and precedent

In England and Wales courts operate a rigid hierarchy of judicial precedents. Every court is bound to follow any decision made by a court above it in the hierarchy. In general, appellate courts (appeal courts) are bound by their own decisions. The diagram below indicates the hierarchy of courts.

Civil cases	**Criminal cases**
European Court of Justice	European Court of Justice
|	|
House of Lords	House of Lords
|	|
Court of Appeal (Civil Division)	Court of Appeal (Criminal Division)
|	|
Divisional Courts	Queens Bench Divisional Court
|	|
High Court	Crown Court
|	|
County Court	Magistrates Court
|	
Magistrates Court	

The European Court of Justice

The highest court affecting the legal system in England and Wales is the European Court of Justice. This has been the case since 1973. For points of European law, a decision made by this court is binding on all other courts in England and Wales. There are still laws unaffected by European Union law and for these the House of Lords is the Supreme Court.

House of Lords

The House of Lords is the most senior court nationally and its decisions bind all other courts in the English legal system. The House of Lords is not bound by its past decisions, even though it will generally follow them.

The main debate about the House of Lords is the extent to which it should follow its own decisions and the ideas regarding this have changed over the years. Originally, the view was that the House of Lords had the right to overrule its own past decisions but this has changed. In one seminal case, *London Street Tramways v London County Council (1898)* The House of Lords held that certainty in the law was more important than the possibility of hardship being caused by the need to follow past decisions. From 1898 to 1966 the House of Lords regarded itself as being completely bound by its own past decisions unless that decision was made in error (*per incuriam*). However, this idea of error referred only to situations where a decision had been made without considering the effect of a relevant statute.

This was felt to be unsatisfactory as the law could not alter to meet changing social conditions and opinions nor could any 'wrong decisions' be changed by the courts. If there was an unsatisfactory decision made by the House of Lords then the only way to change it was by passing an Act of Parliament.

It was realised that the House of Lords should have more flexibility and, in 1966, the Lord Chancellor issued a Practice Statement announcing a change to the rule in London Street Tramways v London County Council, which said as follows:

'Their Lordships regard the use of precedent as an indispensable foundation upon which to decide what is the law and its application in individual cases. It provides at least some degree of certainty upon which individuals can rely in the conduct of their own affairs, as well as a basis for orderly development of legal rules.

Their lordships nevertheless recognise that the rigid adherence to precedent may lead to injustice in a particular case and also unduly restrict the proper development of the law. They propose therefore to modify their present practice and while treating former decisions of this house as normally binding, to depart from a previous decision when it appears right to do so.

In this connection they will bear in mind the danger of disturbing retrospectively the basis on which contracts, settlement of property and fiscal arrangements have been entered into and also the especial need for certainty as to the criminal law. This announcement is not intended to affect the use of precedent elsewhere in this house'

Court of appeal

The court of appeal is next in the hierarchy and has two divisions, civil and criminal. Both of these divisions are bound to follow the decisions of the European Court of Justice and the House of Lords. They must also follow past decisions of their own although there are exceptions to the rule and the Court of Appeal (Criminal Division) is more flexible where it involves the liberty of the subject.

Divisional courts

The three divisional courts, Queens Bench, Chancery and Family are bound by decisions of the European Court of Justice, the House of Lords and the Court of Appeal. The divisional courts are also bound by their own past decisions, although there are some exceptions.

Courts of first instance

This term means any court where the original trial of a case is held. Appeal courts do not hear any original trials only appeals from those trials. Courts of first instance rarely ever create precedents only following decisions of courts above them.

The High Court

The High Court is bound by decisions of all courts above it and in turn it binds the lower courts.

Inferior courts

Inferior courts are the Crown Court, the County Court and the Magistrates Court. They are bound to follow decisions of all higher courts. It is very unlikely that a decision by a lower court can create a precedent. The one exception is that a ruling on a point of law by a judge in a Crown Court will bind the Magistrates Court.

Use of Practice Statement

Since 1966 the Practice Statement has allowed the House of Lords to change the law if it believes that an earlier case was wrongly decided

Distinguishing, overruling and reversing previous decisions

Distinguishing is a method used by a judge to avoid following a past decision which otherwise would have to be followed. It means that the judge finds that the material facts of the case he is following are sufficiently different for him to draw a distinction between the present case and the previous case. He is not then bound by the previous case.

Overruling is where a court in a later case decides that the legal rule in a previous case is wrong. Overruling may occur when a higher court overrules a decision by a lower court, for example the House of Lords overruling a decision by the Court of Appeal.

Reversing is where a court higher up in the hierarchy overturns the decision of a lower court on appeal in the same case.

Advantages and disadvantages of precedent in the law

There are advantages and disadvantages to the way judicial precedent operates in England and Wales.

Advantages

The main advantages to the operation of precedent are:

Certainty
Because the courts follow past decisions, people know what the law is and how it is likely to be applied in their case. Lawyers advise clients on the likely outcome of cases and it also allows people to operate their businesses in the certainty that what they do is within the law.

Consistency and fairness
It is seen as just and fair that similar cases are decided in the same way.

Precision
As the principles of law are set out in actual cases, the law becomes very precise.

Flexibility
There is room for the law to change as the House of Lords can use the Practice Statement to overrule cases.

Time- saving

Precedent can be considered a useful time saving device as where a principle has been established, cases with similar facts are unlikely to go through the lengthy process of litigation.

Disadvantages

Rigidity

The fact that lower courts have to follow decisions of higher courts, together with the fact that the Court of Appeal has to follow its own past decisions, can make the law too inflexible so that bad decisions made in the past can be perpetuated.

Complexity

There are many reported cases and it may be complex and time consuming to find the right case on which to base a decision.

Illogical distinctions

The use of distinguishing to avoid past decisions can lead to illogical distinctions so that some areas of law have become very complex.

Reporting cases

Written law reports have existed in England and Wales since the 13th century. Reports right from the early times were inaccurate and difficult to follow. In 1865 the Incorporated Council of Law was set up, controlled by the courts. Law reports became more accurate and precise, with judgements being noted word for word.

This accuracy of reports was one of the factors in the development of the strict doctrine of precedent. There are also other well established reports today, notably the All England Series (abbreviated to All ER) and the weekly law Reports (WLR). The internet also provides reports, websites such as www. lawreports.co.uk and www.publications.parliament.uk.

2

The Purpose of Criminal Law

Having looked at the development of law and the operations of the legal system we will now turn to criminal law.

The main purposes of criminal law are to:

- Protect individuals and their property from damage or harm
- To preserve order in society
- To punish those who deserve punishment

The most important distinction between civil law and criminal law is that, under criminal law, with which this book deals, the state plays a major role. Criminal law is, in effect, a crime against the state.

Defining a crime

There are varying definitions of a crime but they are all variations on the same theme. Essentially a crime is:

- A conduct forbidden by the state. Punishment is meted out to any person who violates the rules of criminal law. The state enforces those rules.

It is true to say that many offences committed involve breaches of morals, or moral wrongs. However, there are many subtle differences between morality and crime. There are areas of morality which are not crimes, moral wrongs such as adultery or telling of lies. Although these kinds of moral wrongs are offensive to many people the law would not get involved.

The Wolfenden Committee of 1957 came to the conclusion that it is not the function of criminal law to interfere with the private lives of citizens in order to try to impose certain standards of behaviour. It was felt that this should only be done:

To preserve public order and decency to protect the citizen from what is offensive or injurious, and to provide sufficient safeguards against exploitation and corruption of others, particularly those who are especially vulnerable.

Sources of criminal law

Criminal law combines a mix of common law rules and Acts of Parliament. Common law rules are rules that have been laid down over time by judges. However Parliament is now the dominating law making assembly. The sources of criminal law are therefore mixed.

The crimes of murder and manslaughter provide an example of the interaction between the judiciary and Parliament. Until the middle of this century, until the 1965 Murder (Abolition of Death Penalty) Act, murder was punishable by death. After 1965 the death penalty was suspended except for murder or treason. The Crime and Disorder Act 1998 removed the death penalty for treason and piracy.

There is no Act of Parliament that defines murder. This has been developed by the judiciary over the years. Their definition originally stated that death had to occur within a year and a day. In 1996, this definition was abolished with the passing of the Law Reform (Year and a Day Rule) Act 1996.

With regard to voluntary manslaughter, this was originally curtailed by the judges. The Homicide Act 1957 then extended it by reducing the charge from murder to manslaughter where the defendant could demonstrate that he or she was suffering from diminished responsibility at the time of the killing, had been provoked or was the survivor of a suicide pact.

The classification of offences

Offences can be divided into summary offences and indictable offences. Summary offences are more minor offences and indictable more serious. There is a third category that fits in between the former two, triable either way offences.

Summary offences

These offences must first be tried in a Magistrates Court. They are usually always dealt with there and then by magistrates and do not progress to Crown Court. Such cases are:

- Speeding and careless driving
- Minor criminal damage
- Assault and battery
- Assaulting a police officer in the course of his duty
- Drunken driving

Indictable offences

These are more serious or complicated cases that cannot be decided by magistrates. They will be dealt with by the Crown Court. These offences include:

- Rape
- Murder
- Manslaughter
- Robbery
- Arson

The magistrates will decide whether the defendant is remanded on bail or is held in custody. The Bail Act 1976 states that everyone has a general right to bail unless the offence is particularly serious, such as violence or sexual offences. Magistrates must justify their reasoning.

Triable either-way offences

These offences may be tried either summarily or by indictment. If the magistrates decide that it is serious enough to be tried in a Crown Court then the defendant has no say in the matter of where it is tried. However, if the magistrates decide that they can try the case then the defendant can decide whether he wants it tried in the

Magistrates Court or whether it should go to Crown Court. If the defendant decides on a Magistrates Court trial then he will be warned that the case could still go to the Crown Court.

Examples of triable either-way offences include:

- Dangerous driving
- Obtaining property or services by deception
- Theft
- Burglary
- Criminal damage over £5,000

Elements of a crime

The burden of proof in criminal law

In all cases, before a person can be convicted of a wrong against the State, the jury must be convinced by the prosecution that he has committed the crime of which he is accused. The prosecution must establish the burden of proof beyond all reasonable doubt.

One case that clarified this was Woolmington v DPP 1935. In this case, the defendant claimed that he took a gun with him to the home of the victim's mother, with no criminal intention, but to demonstrate to his estranged wife that he planned to commit suicide if she didn't return to him. The gun, so the defendant alleged, went off by accident and he shot his estranged wife and was convicted of murder.

The House of Lords overturned the judgement on appeal stating that it was not necessary for the defendant to prove his innocence and that the shooting was accidental, but for the prosecution to prove guilt by establishing that the killing had been intentional.

Establishing criminal liability

The prosecution in a case, when trying to establish criminal liability, will usually have to prove several things:

- that the defendant has actually committed the crime in question. This is known as the *actus reus* of the offence

- that the defendant had committed the wrong with the degree of blameworthiness required by the law, with the necessary 'guilty mind'. This element of the offence is known as the *mens rea*

The *actus reus* of a crime

The establishment of *actus reus* or the existence of *actus reus* is essential for criminal liability to be proven. Each crime has its own *actus reus,* laid down either by judges or statute. An *actus reus* of theft, for example, under the Theft Act 1968, arises where a party 'appropriates property belonging to another'. In many cases, the actions and motivations of the accused will be plain to see but others can be more complex, as we will see.

Conduct of the accused

In many cases, the conduct of the accused may be enough to show the *actus reus* has been committed. A clear case of this is perjury, or lying under oath. Another example is theft. Once a person has taken property belonging to someone else, the *actus reus* of the offence will have been established.

If the accused has done this intentionally then it will be deemed that he will also have the necessary guilty mind.

Result or consequence

For the commission of some crimes it is necessary to demonstrate the result or consequence of the crime as well as conduct. For example, in the crime of murder, the violent act must have resulted in an unlawful killing.

An omission

In English law an person will not be found to be criminally liable merely because he has failed to act. This was outlined in the nineteenth century by Stephen LJ when he stated:

It is not a crime to cause death or bodily injury, even intentionally, by any omission.

Stephen L J went on to describe a situation where a person sees another person drowning but does not reach out to help him, although by doing so this would have saved the person life. This is not a crime. There are a few exceptions to the rule. They include the following situations:

- A limited number of statutory provisions create liability for omissions. Under the Road Traffic Act 1988, a person failing to provide a breath test as required is liable as is someone failing to give details to someone entitled to receive them after a road traffic accident and someone failing to report an accident as required. It is also a statutory offence to fail to provide a child with adequate food, shelter or medical help, under the Children's and Young Person's Act 1933.
- Where there is a contractual duty to act in a certain way. There may be a duty under a contract to behave in a specific way. One such case demonstrating this was Pittwood 1902 where an employee was employed to guard a level crossing. The guard opened a gate to allow a cart through but failed to close the gate. A few minutes later, a passing train hit a hay cart crossing the track killing the cart driver.
- Where there is a duty imposed by law. The judges have imposed liability for omissions in certain situations and circumstances. In Dytham 1979, a police officer stood by and watched a man being kicked to death. The Court of Appeal upheld the criminal conviction for misconduct in a public offence. A party may also be found guilty of failing to act if there is a duty imposed on him by virtue of the special relationship between him and the victim. One such case was Instan 1893 where a niece failed to get help for her aunt with whom

she was living. The aunt contracted gangrene in her leg and died and the niece was held guilty of manslaughter. Two other areas where omission implies liability are where the defendant has voluntarily accepted responsibility for the other and where there is liability under a continuous act.

The *Mens Rea* of a crime

In most cases it will be necessary that the defendant has committed the act with the relevant *mens rea* or the degree of blameworthiness required by the offence. Some offences, such as the offence of strict liability, outlined later do not require fault to be proved.

Different degrees of *mens rea*

This varies depending on the seriousness of the offence. In the most serious criminal offences the prosecution will usually have to prove a high degree of blameworthiness. The defendant will only be held to be guilty if it can be proved that he fully intended to commit the crime.

Crimes of specific intent

Murder is a crime of specific intent where the accused will only be convicted by the jury if they are convinced that he meant to kill or cause grievous bodily harm. Intention is also needed for theft crimes. The accused will not be convicted unless it can be demonstrated that he took property with the intention of permanently depriving the other person of it.

Crime of basic intent

There are certain crimes that do not require such a high degree of fault to be demonstrated. They can be committed either with intention or recklessly. Such offences are assault, battery, actual bodily harm and malicious wounding.

Intention

A jury has to decide whether the accused carried out a crime with intent. There is no clear definition of intention. They can only arrive at this conclusion through examining all the evidence. Judges have stated that intention to do something should not be confused with the desire or motive to do something. We might contemplate doing something but we cannot be tried for it unless we actually do it. Cunliffe v Goodman 1950 highlighted this when it was stated that intention is a state of affairs *'that a person does more than merely contemplate'*.

The intention to commit a crime should not be confused with motivation, as this is secondary. Although the defendant might feel justified in acting as he did. However, the fact that intention exists means that the *mens rea* will have been established. The motive is irrelevant.

Direct intention

In a lot of cases, it will not be difficult for the jurors to decide whether the defendant had the required *mens rea* as the circumstances are quite obvious. One such example might be a suicide bomber whose intentions are directly obvious. If such a person survived an attack, which is highly unlikely, then a jury would not have much problem in finding the necessary intention.

Oblique intention

This arises where the intention of the offender is different to the result. This might arise for example where a person decides to cause damage to property motivated through revenge. However, when carrying out that revenge he inadvertently kills several people. This was not his intention but it happened.

The position on this is not clear and the House of Lords expressed an opinion in the case of Woollin 1998. The Law Lords stated that it was clearly the jury's task to determine whether or not the defendant intended to kill or cause harm. In cases of oblique intent however, the jury should be directed that they are not entitled to find the necessary intention unless they feel certain that death or serious bodily harm was a virtually certain result of a defendant's action and the defendant had appreciated this fact.

Recklessness

For many offences, it is not necessary to demonstrate a high degree of blameworthiness but only to show the accused was reckless.

Recklessness is the taking of unjustifiable risk. Here, we will look at two types of recklessness, or differing degrees of recklessness:

- It is argued by some that a defendant is only liable if he had actually foreseen that he was taking an unjustifiable risk. If he had not foreseen the risk then he is not liable
- The other belief is that the defendant could be convicted if he ought to have foreseen such a risk

The types of recklessness outlined above are known respectively as Cunningham and Caldwell recklessness, so called after cases involving those named people.

Cunningham recklessness

This was established in the case of Cunningham 1957. The action of 'malicious intent' was central to this case. The defendant stole money from a gas meter and in the process tore the meter from the wall and left the pipes exposed. Gas seeped through into next door and affected the woman residing there. Cunningham was convicted but successfully appealed. It was held that the judge had misdirected the jury by stating that 'malicious' meant 'wicked' instead of expanding on the more precise legal meaning.

The Appeal Court stated that when the word 'malicious' was used in a statute, it was necessary to establish that the defendant had either intended to cause the harm in question or had foreseen that such an event would occur.

Using the above as a test, Cunningham could only be convicted if he knew the risk from the gas but went on to take it nevertheless. It was not enough that he ought to have foreseen a risk. The test was subjective.

Caldwell recklessness

The above was the position until the cases of Caldwell and Lawrence in 1982.

In Caldwell 1982 the defendant had been engaged to work for the proprietor of a hotel but was dismissed and felt a grievance against the owner. Drunk, Caldwell broke a window and started a fire on the ground floor. This was discovered and put out quickly and no harm was done with the exception of minor damage. Caldwell admitted to the charge of criminal damage but not a more serious charge of causing criminal damage with the intent to endanger life or being reckless as to whether life would be endangered. He was found guilty and given three years imprisonment.

The case went to appeal, to the House of Lords, where Lord Diplock gave the main speech, changing the law on recklessness, in relation to the crime of criminal damage. He stated:

That the only person who knows what the accused's mental processes were at the time of committing the crime is the accused himself and probably not even he can recall them accurately when the rage or excitement under which he acted has passed or he has sobered up if he were under the influence of drink at the end of the relevant time.

Lord Diplock decided that a person is reckless under the Criminal Damage Act 1971 if:

1. He does an act which in fact creates an obvious risk that property will be destroyed or damaged, and
2. when he does the act he either has not given any thought to the possibility of there being any such risk or has recognised that there was some risk involved and has nonetheless gone on to do it.

Caldwell's appeal was dismissed and a wider test of recklessness emerged.

Negligence

Negligence occurs when a person behaves or acts in such a way that falls below the standard expected of a reasonable person in the same situation as the accused. Negligence often incurs liability in civil law but there are certain circumstances where a criminal act is also committed.

The distinction between recklessness and negligence is seen as the former being the deliberate taking of an unjustifiable risk whilst the latter is inadvertent risk taking.

Criminal negligence

Criminal negligence can be seen in dangerous driving and causing death by dangerous driving. In addition to driving offences, any grossly negligent behaviour that leads to death may result in a manslaughter charge.

Transferred malice

If a defendant has the *mens rea* for one offence, it can be transferred to another offence of the same type. One case that illustrates this is Latimer 1886 in which the defendant, a soldier, hit a customer in a pub with his belt after being attacked by the other person. The belt rebounded off the victim and hit a woman in the face wounding her. The court held that the *mens rea* from the first attack could be transferred to the other.

Strict liability

There are numerous offences, quite often of a regulatory nature, which have been created as offences of strict liability. Most have been laid out by statute but there are also common law examples such as public nuisance and libel offences.

If an offence is one of strict liability then the defendant may be held criminally liable without any proof of fault on his part.

An early case of strict liability without fault is that of Prince 1875. The defendant was charged under s55 Offences Against The Person Act 1861, with unlawfully taking an unmarried girl under the age of 16 out of the possession of her parents. Prince was found guilty despite the fact that the girl looked much older than her

13 years and had convinced Prince that she was 18. Liability arose when Prince committed the act.

Different types of strict liability offences

Regulatory offences

There are many of these. The case of the London Borough of Harrow v Shah and Shah 2000 involved the defendants being charged with selling a lottery ticket to a person under 16 despite the fact that they had not been present when the transaction took place. Notices were also put up in the store. The magistrates dismissed the charge and the local authority took the case to appeal. The Divisional Court of Queen's Bench Division allowed this appeal stating that there was strict liability as the National Lottery Act 1993 and its corresponding regulations was strict and allowed no defence of 'reasonable diligence'.

More serious criminal offences

In relation to more serious offences where the outcome for the accused can be far more serious, the House of Lords is far less ready to impose strict liability.

One case which emphasises this is Sweet v Parsley 1970, where a teacher leased a farmhouse near Oxford, which she then rented to students. She kept a room for her own occasional use. The students used drugs on the premises and this resulted in Sweet being convicted of being involved in the management of premises which were being used for the smoking of cannabis under the Dangerous Drugs Act 1965. The court of first instance (the originating court) and the

Queens Bench Division decided that she was strictly liable. The case went to the House of Lords.

Lord Reid made a clear distinction between regulatory criminal offences and ones which he decided were 'truly criminal acts'. Whereas the imposition of strict liability might well be appropriate for the former type of offence Lord Reid felt that there was a strong presumption that *mens rea* was needed for the latter type of crime. Sweets conviction was squashed in this case. Following this case, the Dangerous Drugs Act 1965 was replaced by the Misuse of Drugs Act and the section corresponding to the one affecting Sweet was replaced by one requiring knowledge before liability is imposed.

3

Unlawful killing

Murder

The distinction between murder and manslaughter

The most common definition of murder is 'the killing of a human being with malice aforethought'. This basically means that a person intended to kill another, the killing was pre-meditated.

Manslaughter can be either voluntary or involuntary. Voluntary manslaughter arises where the definition of murder seems to have been satisfied but one of three defences can be pleaded. These are diminished responsibility, provocation and the survivor of a suicide pact. Involuntary manslaughter occurs where there is no malice aforethought, no intention but a death occurs because of an involuntary act or an act of gross negligence. We will be discussing manslaughter further on in the book.

Murder and manslaughter share the same *actus reus* which is the unlawful killing of a human being. The *mens rea* for murder and voluntary manslaughter is killing with intent whilst the *mens rea* for involuntary manslaughter will vary and will be explored later.

Murder

As we have seen, murder is a common law offence and not an offence laid down by statute. If convicted of murder the judge will impose a mandatory life sentence.

The definition of murder

The famous judge and former Lord Chief Justice of England, Coke, set out his early definition of murder. This is said to arise where:

A man of sound memory and the age of discretion unlawfully killed within any county of the realm any reasonable creature in rerum natura under the King's peace, with malice aforethought, either expressed by the party or implied by law, so that the party wounded or hurt etc die of the wound or hurt etc within a year and a day after the same.

As with many areas of the law this early definition has changed over the years.

Year and a day rule

In 1996, the 'year and a day' rule was removed. This timescale had been set down in earlier times in order to determine whether death was caused by the act of murder or whether it was later illness or accident. As medical techniques have changed it has become easier to determine causes of death and there were calls for the abolition of the rule as no longer relevant.

The Law Reform (Year and a Day) Act 1996 reformed the law and the year and a day rule ceased to be relevant.

Current definition of murder

The current definition of murder can be said to be ' the unlawful killing of an human being under the Queens peace with malice aforethought'. The killing must be the result of an unlawful act and certain acts are not considered criminal. For example, killings by execution, killings by the armed forces or police in the line of duty and certain deaths (in very limited circumstances) accelerated by the medical profession are not considered to be unlawful.

The victim (obviously) must be human. Murder or manslaughter is not relevant in law if the victim is an animal. Newborn babies which are barely recognisable as a human being are covered by the law although obviously the debate over this is strong and ongoing. The courts must decide when life begins. Normally, a foetus must have been expelled from the mother's womb and have an independent existence. One case which emphasised this was Rance v Mid-Downs Health authority 1991 where it was stated that a baby is capable of being born alive if it can breathe through its own lungs.

An attack on an unborn child, either by the mother herself or by another would usually only result in a charge of abortion or child destruction. However, if damage is occasioned to the unborn child and it is subsequently born then a charge of manslaughter can be brought (Attorney General's reference (no 3 of 1994)).

Under the Queen's peace

Most victims of murder would come within this category.

Malice aforethought

This is an old expression and misleading. The actual words 'malice aforethought' merely means that the accused intended to cause death or grievous bodily harm. Although there existed some doubt as to whether the intention to cause grievous bodily harm was sufficient intention to murder the case of Cunningham 1982 made clear that the intention to cause serious harm was enough.

If a person intends to take the life of another he is said to have express malice. If the intention is to cause serious bodily harm then this is implied malice

Chain of causation

The death of another must have been caused by the unlawful death of the defendant. The defendant does not have to have been directly responsible for the actual final act that resulted in the death of another person but will still be liable for the homicide because he was responsible for the chain of events that led up to it.

Courts look at several issues when deciding the guilt or otherwise of the defendant:

- Did the conduct of the accused cause the resulting harm (what was the factual cause of death?)
- Was the defendant also liable in law?

When deciding on the factual cause of death the courts will use the 'but for' test, i.e. but for the act of the defendant, the death would not have occurred.

After initially satisfying the test of factual causation, the courts still need to be shown that the defendant's act was a significant cause of the death and that no act in between, or intervening act, had broken the chain of causation. The defendant can escape liability if he or she can demonstrate that some other act had caused the death.

Several cases highlight the difficulty of establishing intervening acts. In Pagett 1983, the accused was being chased by police and had then taken his pregnant girlfriend captive after injuring her mother and stepfather. He used his girlfriend as a human shield when trying to escape and in the process aimed a shot at the police who in turn fired back killing the girlfriend. The defendant was found guilty of her manslaughter and tried to get this charge overturned by stating that the jury had been misdirected in saying that he was the cause of the death instead of the police officer.

The Court of Appeal found that there was no misdirection. Patently the chain of events were set in motion by the accused.

In Williams 1992, the prosecution had claimed that the deceased person had jumped from a car because he was in fear of being robbed. To support this, it was alleged that his wallet had flown into the air as he jumped. The victim had 'hitched' a lift from the defendants. He had jumped out five miles on and had been killed. The defendants were originally held to be liable for the death but appealed.

The Court of Appeal stated that the conduct of the victim had to be proportionate to the threat of harm and quashed the conviction.

Voluntary manslaughter

This crime is similar to murder in that an unlawful homicide has taken place with the intention to kill, or malice aforethought. However, special circumstances exist which allow for the less serious charge of involuntary manslaughter. As stated, there are three defences to murder which can result in voluntary manslaughter: diminished responsibility, provocation and survival of a suicide pact.

Diminished responsibility

Section 2 of the 1957 Homicide Act states that a person may be found guilty of voluntary manslaughter rather than murder if he was suffering from an abnormality of mind caused by an inside source that substantially affected his responsibility for his actions.

Section 2 of the act puts the burden of proof on the defendant. He will have to prove his abnormality of mind on a balance of probabilities and in general must be the one to raise the defence.

If the plea of voluntary manslaughter is to be used in an appeal then strong evidence will need to be shown for this to succeed.

'Abnormality of mind' is defined as a state of mind a reasonable man would find abnormal. Inside source is seen as an abnormality which must be caused by 'arrested or retarded development of mind or any inherent causes or induced by disease or injury'.

The abnormality of mind must be demonstrated to be greater than that experienced by an ordinary person. There must be medical evidence in support of the abnormality.

Provocation

This defence may be available if the loss of control which led to the act was caused by provocation of another(s).

S3 of the Homicide Act 1957 states:

'Where, on a charge of murder, there is evidence on which the jury can find that the person charged was provoked (whether by things done or things said or both together) to lose his self

control, the question whether the provocation was enough to make a reasonable man do as he did shall be left to be determined by the jury'

Evidence of provocation

The judge will decide whether there is enough evidence to be put before the jury. Provocation can arise from either things done or said. The words or actions do not need to have come from the deceased nor need they be directed at the defendant.

In Pearson 1992, the victim (father) had persecuted and ill treated the accused person's brother. The Court of Appeal decided that this could be used as a defence after he killed his father with a sledgehammer.

If the accused is the one who has started the trouble, this will be regarded as 'self induced' provocation. A case which illustrates this is Johnson 1989. The accused started an argument in a night club, during which he made threats to the victim and his girlfriend. A fight started and the victim was fatally stabbed. The accused alleged he was provoked by the fear of being glassed by the victim but the judge did not put this matter before the jury.

The Court of Appeal allowed the defendants appeal, despite the fact that he was the one who had started the trouble.

Loss of self-control

In addition to being provoked, the defendant must show that the provocation was strong enough to make him lose his self-control.

The standard definition of provocation arose in the case of Duffy 1949. In this case, an abused wife killed her husband in bed after a quarrel. The definition in this case allows the defence to be used where the provoking event has caused:

A sudden and temporary loss of self-control rendering the accused so subject to passion as to make him or her, for the moment, not a master of his mind.

There does not need to be a complete loss of control to the extent that the accused does not know what he is doing.

Reasonable man acting in a similar way

Although this may seem a simple proposition, it is in fact quite a complex area. Who or what exactly, is a reasonable man? The House of Lords, in Camplin 1978 stated that the reasonable man is said to be a normal man with normal attributes. In this case, a 15 year old boy had been drinking and went with an older man to the latters house where the boy was forcibly subjected to a homosexual assault. When he expressed shame at what had happened the older man allegedly taunted him. The boy attacked him and killed him with a pan. He was convicted of murder after a direction from the judge about a reasonable man.

The House of Lords decided that, while certain of the boy's characteristics should not be taken into account, such as his drunkenness and excitability, other characteristics such as age, could be. The question for the jury therefore was whether a reasonable youth with similar characteristics would have acted in the same way. The appeal against murder was upheld.

Now, however, following numerous cases and deliberations, particularly Smith and Morgan 2000, a reasonable man is seen to be a reasonable person sharing similar characteristics to the accused. Basically, age, physical characteristics and mental characteristics may be taken into account when measuring the effects of provocation.

In the case of Smith and Morgan 2000, the defendant and the victim had been drinking, indeed were both alcoholics and long-standing drinking partners. During an argument over an alleged theft of Smith's tools, Smith became furious over the others ongoing denials. He stabbed his friend to death with a kitchen knife. At his trial he put forward the defences of diminished responsibility and provocation. He claimed to have a depressive illness that affected his actions.

The trial judge directed the jury that the characteristics of mental impairment could only be brought forward when deciding on the gravity of the provocation, they were not relevant to the reasonable man's loss of self control. The accused was found guilty of murder and, on appeal, the Court of Appeal overturned the verdict and substituted a verdict of manslaughter. The House of Lords agreed that the trial judge had erred by telling the jury that the effect of the defendant's depression on his powers of self-control was not material.

The survivor of a suicide pact

Suicide was a crime until the Suicide Act of 1961 was passed. In addition, before the Suicide Act, if another person was involved in the suicide and survived then he or she would be charged with the murder of the person that did not survive.

Suicide is no longer a crime and those that aid and abet suicide are treated more leniently than they were.

Under s4(1) of the 1957 Homicide Act, if two or more people enter into a suicide pact and one or more survives, that survivor is charged with manslaughter and not murder. The burden of proving a suicide pact is on the accused. A suicide pact, under the 1957 Act is defined as:

an agreement between two or more persons which has as its objects the death of all parties to it.

Infanticide

This is set out in the Infanticide Act 1938. It is an alternative charge to the charge of murder. It is only available to a woman who has killed her child, provided the child is under the age of 12 months. The woman must provide evidence that she did the killing while the balance of her mind was disturbed because she had not fully recovered from the effect of giving birth or because of breast feeding the child. The prosecution must disprove this.

Abortion

Under s58 Offences Against the Person Act 1861 it is an offence to try to procure a miscarriage. The offence can be committed by the woman herself or by another by unlawfully administering any poison or other noxious thing or unlawfully using an instrument or any other means. It is not necessary to show that a miscarriage has actually been caused.

By s1(1) of the Abortion Act 1967, there is no offence if the pregnancy is terminated by a registered medical practitioner where two doctors are of the opinion that:

- the pregnancy has not exceeded the 24th week and that the continuance of the pregnancy involves greater risk of injury to health of the woman or any existing children of her family than if the pregnancy was terminated; or
- at any time during the pregnancy if the termination is necessary to prevent grave permanent injury to the physical or mental health of the pregnant woman; or
- at any time during the pregnancy if the continuance of the pregnancy would involve

greater risk to the life of the pregnant woman than if the pregnancy was terminated; or

- there is a substantial risk that if the child were born it would suffer from a serious physical or mental handicap.

Involuntary manslaughter

With both murder and voluntary manslaughter, an intention to kill or cause grievous bodily harm has to be proven. This is not the case with involuntary manslaughter.

With involuntary manslaughter, it is enough that the defendant has committed an unlawful and dangerous act and death has resulted, or that someone has died through gross negligence on the part of the accused.

There are two types of involuntary manslaughter: Constructive manslaughter and manslaughter by gross negligence.

Constructive manslaughter

Constructive manslaughter is also known as 'constructive act manslaughter'. This is because the defendant has caused the death of another by an unlawful and dangerous act. There is a clear distinction between this form of manslaughter and gross negligence manslaughter as outlined in the case of Larkin 1943 by Humphreys J:

If a person is engaged in doing a lawful act, and in the course of doing that lawful act behaves so negligently as to cause the death of some other person, then it is for the jury to say, upon consideration of the whole of the facts of the case, whether the negligence proved against the accused person amounts to manslaughter, and it is the duty of the presiding judge to tell them that it will not amount to manslaughter unless the negligence is of a very high degree... That is where the act is lawful. Where the act which a person is engaged in is unlawful, then if at the same time it is a dangerous act, that is an act which is likely to injure another person, and quite inadvertently he causes the death of that other person by that act, then he is guilty of manslaughter.

Three elements therefore have to be established before a person is liable for constructive manslaughter:

- An unlawful act must have been committed
- The act must have caused death
- The unlawful act must have been dangerous

Unlawful act

When a person is charged with constructive manslaughter this is often in the context of assaulting another person or persons. It is not a viable defence to argue that the defendant did not intend to injure the other person.

One case illustrating this is Larkin 1943, as described above where the accused had discovered his mistress with another man and had taken a razor to the scene. Although he alleged that he intended to only frighten the man he in fact stated that his drunken mistress had fallen onto the razor and cut her throat. Notwithstanding this claim, the conviction for unlawful manslaughter was upheld because an assault had been committed which cause the death of the woman.

For any liability to be established the prosecution has the task of establishing that an unlawful act took place. Two cases illustrate where this was not proved. In Lamb 1967, the accused person and his friend were playing with a revolver. The gun had two bullets in it none of which were opposite the barrel. The defendant believed the gun was safe and pulled the trigger with the unfortunate result that the gun fired a live round and killed the other. The Court of Appeal quashed the conviction as it believed that an unlawful act had not been committed.

In the other case Arioboke 1988, the victim was fearful of violence from another man, with whom he had had ongoing bad relations. The accused had been peering into a train carriage looking for the victim, the victim had panicked and ran across railway lines trying to escape and had been electrocuted. Arioboke was convicted of manslaughter but the Court of Appeal quashed the conviction on the grounds that there had been no actual assault.

In addition to the unlawful act, death must have arisen as a result of it. It does not have to be the sole cause of it but must have significantly contributed to it. There must, however, have been no other intervening act to contribute to it. Although the act was originally seen as being directed against the victim in the case of Mitchell

1983, it was determined that an act intended for another person could, under the doctrine of transferred malice, be classed as being directed against the victim. In this case, the accused had tried to push ahead in the queue at a post office and was punched in the mouth by another man. A second punch or push caused the victim of the attack to fall against a woman who broke her leg. Following complications she died and the accused was convicted of manslaughter but appealed.

The Court of Appeal had to decide whether the person at whom the act is directed must also be the person who dies. Staughton J stated:

We can see no reason of policy for holding that an act calculated to harm A cannot be manslaughter if it in fact kills B. The criminality of the doer of the act is precisely the same whether it is A or B who dies.

Another case, Goodfellow 1986 took this further and decided that the accused could still be liable whether or not the act was directed against a person or not. In this case, the accused was being harassed in his council house and wanted to move. He knew the chances of moving were very slim and set fire to his flat to help facilitate the move. His fire was intended to seem as though the house had been petrol bombed hoping that this would lead to re-housing. However, such was the blaze that Goodfellow's wife, son and son's girlfriend all died in the fire.

The Court of Appeal upheld the conviction for manslaughter even though the unlawful act of arson was not specifically directed at the people who died.

Act must also be dangerous

For constructive manslaughter to arise, the act has to also be dangerous. Whether it is dangerous is an objective decision, it must be an act that a reasonable man would regard as dangerous.

The case of Church 1996 where the defendant panicked after hitting a woman who had mocked his love making abilities, illustrates this. The defendant believed the woman was dead and threw her in the river where she was drowned. The Court of Appeal upheld the conviction for manslaughter stating:

An unlawful act causing the death of another cannot, simply because it is an unlawful act, render a manslaughter verdict inevitable. For such a verdict inexorably to follow, the unlawful act must be such as all sober and reasonable people would inevitably recognize must subject the other person to, at least, the risk of some harm resulting therefrom, albeit it not serious harm.

Manslaughter by gross negligence

Manslaughter by gross negligence is caused by an act of negligence that has caused the death of another. One case illustrating this is Adomako 1995. In this case Doctor Adamako's actions of negligence caused his patients death. Lord Mackay decided that liability for this type of manslaughter will arise where the jury decides that:

Having regard to the risk of death involved, the conduct of the defendant was so bad in all the circumstances as to amount in their judgement to a criminal act or omission.

In Adomako, it was decided by the House of Lords that the gross negligence test is the correct one to use in all cases where a duty of care has been broken.

However, the principles of civil and criminal law do not always sit well together. The case of Wacker 2003 demonstrated this. This case involved the bodies of 58 illegal immigrants and two survivors which were found in a lorry at Dover. The deaths arose because the container was sealed from the outside preventing oxygen from entering. The defendant was convicted of 58 counts of manslaughter by gross negligence and appealed. He argued that because the illegal immigrants had shared the same purpose as him, i.e. to gain illegal entry to the UK, he did not owe them a duty of care.

The Court of Appeal rejected this argument. It decided that the public policy issues relating to civil law were different to criminal law and even where there was an underlying illegal purpose this did not prevent criminal liability arising. The conviction in this case was upheld.

Corporate manslaughter

A corporation is a legal entity with directors managing and shareholders supposedly controlling. The corporation can range from a large PLC to a small company.

Originally it was decided that a corporation cannot be criminally liable on the basis that a personal appearance was needed in court and this could not be the case with a corporate body. However, following the passing of the Criminal Justice Act 1925 it was decided that a representative of the company can now appear in court.

A company can be liable for manslaughter in one of the following ways:

1. When the principle of vicarious liability is invoked. A company can be held vicariously liable under certain limited circumstances for the actions of its employees. In the case of Mousell Ltd v London and North Western Railway Limited 1917 the company was held liable for evading freight charges.
2. Where a statute expressly makes a corporation liable. The Interpretation Act 1978 states that the word 'person' includes a body of persons corporate or unincorporated, which includes companies and partnerships.
3. Where the doctrine of identification is used. The general rule is that a company cannot be convicted of a crime for which it cannot be sentenced, so it can only be convicted for an offence for which a fine can be imposed. It could not therefore be held liable for murder.

However, in a ruling in P&O European Ferries, it was decided that a company could be held liable for manslaughter. In this case, the Herald of Free Enterprise, a roll-on roll-off ferry sank just outside Zeebrugge harbour in 1987. The ferry had departed from port with its bow doors open and the ship capsized, killing nearly 200 passengers. It was the job of the assistant bosun to ensure that the doors were shut but he was asleep at the time. The captain was responsible for the ship setting sail safely but he had no way of confirming that the doors were shut. These two employees were charged with manslaughter, along with directors of the company and the actual company itself. The case against all people involved collapsed. The defendants had argued that a killing had to be one human killing another. Turner J disagreed but did acknowledge that clear liability in the case of a corporate entity would be difficult to establish. He stated:

A company may be vicariously liable for the negligent acts or omissions of its servants and agents, but for a company to be criminally liable for manslaughter it is required that the mens rea and actus reus of manslaughter should be established not only against those who acted for the company but against those who were identified as the embodiment of the company itself.

Where an offence requires *mens rea* there has to be some way of finding this in a company structure, because a company has no mind. In relation to lesser crimes the courts have overcome this by developing the doctrine of identification. This is achieved by looking for personnel in the company who are said to be the directing mind and will of the organisation.

In H L Bolton (Engineering) Co Ltd v T J Graham and Sons Ltd 1957, Lord Denning, likening a company to a human body, interpreted the doctrine of identification as follows:

It has a brain and nerve centre which controls what it does. It also has hands which control the tools and acts in accordance with directions from the centre. Some of the people in the company are mere servants and agents who are nothing more than hands to do the work and cannot be said to represent the will or mind. Others are directors and managers who represent the directing mind and will of the company and control what it does. The state of mind of these managers is the state and mind of the company and is treated by the law as such.

4

Non-Fatal offences against the person

Assault

An assault, or common assault, arises when the person accused of assault intentionally or recklessly causes the victim to apprehend immediate and unlawful violence. In the case of Ireland 1998, the House of Lords confirmed the above definition. If the offence is assault however, this concerns the inflicting of actual harm.

Assault and battery are separate offences and are contained within s39 of the Criminal Justice Act 1988, which repealed s47 of the Offences against the Person Act 1861. The Criminal Justice Act 1988 states that common assault and battery are to be treated as summary offences with a maximum sentence of six months.

Actus reus of assault

The actus reus of assault occurs when the accused causes the victim to apprehend immediate and unlawful violence. No force need be applied. Any conduct which causes the victim to believe that he or she is to be assaulted can amount to an assault.

In the case of Wilson 1955, Lord Goddard stated that words alone can constitute an assault. In the case of Ireland 1988 the House of Lords also decided that silence can amount to an assault. In this case, the accused terrorised women with silent phone calls.

The threat of assault

The victim must believe that immediate violence is about to be inflicted on him, although the courts will interpret this liberally. Provide the victim believes that he might be subjected to immediate violence, the fear need not be completely rational. In Smith v Chief Superintendent of Woking Police Station 1983, it was stated 'When one is in a state of terror, one is very often unable to analyse precisely what one is frightened of as likely to happen next. In this case, the victim was frightened by the accused, who was staring at her through the windows of her home. The defence in this case argued that the action could not have constituted assault because all windows and doors were locked. The Appeal Court held that it was enough that the woman felt herself to be in danger of having violence inflicted on her.

Mens rea of assault

This is satisfied when the defendant intends to cause the victim to apprehend immediate physical violence or does this recklessly.

Battery

This offence arises when the defendant intentionally or recklessly applies unlawful physical force to another person. The difference between assault and battery is that an assault is committed where the victim believes that he is likely to be subjected to harm and a battery takes place only where force is applied.

The law starts with the assumption that an individual has the right to be protected from molestation. In the case of Collins v Wilcock 1984, Goff L J stated' the fundamental principle, plain and incontestable, is that every person's body is inviolate'.

The above also applies to the police when apprehending a person. They are not allowed to grab or touch a person unless making an arrest. The touching of clothing can also constitute an assault. In the case of Thomas 1985 the rubbing of a girl's skirt was held to amount to battery.

Not all touching is unlawful. In Collins v Wilcock, it was noted:

Most of the physical contacts of ordinary life are not actionable because they are implicitly consented by all who move in society and so expose themselves to risk of bodily contact.

One case which illustrates this is Donnelly v Jackman 1970, where the court held that the officer in question did not commit a battery when he tapped on the other's shoulder to attract attention. Obviously, it is a question of degree.

Indirect battery

Battery need not be directly inflicted on the victim. Scott v Shepherd 1773, illustrated this. In this civil case, the court held that the defendant had committed a battery when he threw an illegal squib into a market place. Two people picked it up and threw it away and it injured one of them. In Martin 1881, the defendant placed an iron bar across an exit in a theatre, turned off the lights and shouted 'fire'. In the panic that followed several people were injured. The defendants conviction for grievous bodily harm was upheld.

The *actus reus and mens rea* of battery

The *actus reus* consists of the application of unlawful physical force on another. The *mens rea* is satisfied when the defendant intends to carry out such an act or is reckless about whether force will be applied.

Consent as a defence

If the alleged victim has given consent to the alleged crime committed against him then no offence will have been committed.

However, the consent must be one that the law recognises as a valid one. These circumstances are limited. In Coney 1882, the courts held that a bare-fist prize fight was illegal, despite the agreement of the parties. In another case, Leach 1969, it was held that the defendants were guilty of assault, even though the victim had consented to being crucified on Hampstead Heat.

Consent may be available 'for properly conducted games and sports, lawful chastisement or correction, reasonable surgical interference, dangerous exhibitions etc'. Practical joking and consent to minor harm in sexual activities are also limited defences.

Lord Templeman stated that in cases where no actual bodily harm had been caused, the consent of the person affected stops him from complaining. He also added that Parliament, under the Sexual Offences Act 1967 had permitted homosexual activities in private between consenting adults. However, he refused to accept the contention of the accused that their sexual appetites could only be satisfied by inflicting serious harm on another:

sado-masochism is not only concerned with sex. It is also concerned with violence. The evidence discloses that the practices of the appellants were unpredictably dangerous and degrading to mind and body and were developed with increasing barbarity and taught to persons whose consents were dubious or worthless.

The message is clear in this summing up. He added ' I am not prepared to invent a defence of consent for sado-masochistic encounters which breed and glorify cruelty and which result in offences under sections 47 and 20 of the Act of 1861.

In summary, the current position on consent in cases of assault and battery is as follows:

- It can be a defence, in certain and appropriate cases of ordinary assault and battery
- It will not usually be a defence in cases of actual and grievous bodily harm
- It will not be available to those who transmit sexual diseases even if the other has consented to intercourse
- It could be available in the case of sexually transmitted diseases if the defendant has clearly accepted the risk.

Actual Bodily Harm

Section 47 of the Offences Against Persons Act 1861 covers actual bodily harm. The act does not define what constitutes actual bodily harm although case law has developed this. The offence is a triable either way offence and there is a maximum sentence of five-years if the case is tried in the Crown Court. If the magistrates agree and the defendant chooses a Magistrates Court trial then the case can be dealt with summarily.

Actual bodily harm is a form of aggravated assault. Before it is decided that the victim has suffered harm then it is necessary to establish that he has been subject to either assault or battery

Defining actual bodily harm

In the case of Miller 1954, the term 'actual bodily harm' was said to include 'any hurt or injury calculated to interfere with the health and comfort of the victim'. In the case of Chan-Fook 1994, the Court of Appeal stated that 'actual bodily harm'

are three words in the English language which require no elaboration and in the ordinary course should not receive any. The word 'harm' is a synonym for 'injury'. The word 'actual' indicates that the injury should not be so trivial as to be wholly insignificant...The body of the victim includes all parts of his body, including his organs, nervous system and brain. Bodily injury therefore may include injury to any of those parts of his body responsible for his mental and other faculties.

Malicious wounding or grievous bodily harm

Section 20 of the OAPA 1861 states that: 'whosoever shall unlawfully and maliciously wound or inflict any grievous bodily harm upon any person, either with or without any weapon or instrument shall be guilty of an offence'. The maximum punishment for this offence is five years.

Malicious wounding or grievous bodily harm is further defined under s18 of the OAPA 1861, which has been amended by the Criminal Law Act 1967. This section states:

'Whosoever shall unlawfully and maliciously by any means whatsoever wound or cause any grievous bodily harm to

another person...with intent to do some grievous bodily harm...or with the intent to resist or prevent the lawful apprehension or detainer of any person, shall be guilty of an offence'.

The maximum sentence for a s18 offence is life imprisonment. This distinguishes it from s20 offence. In addition, the harm cannot have been inflicted recklessly, there must have been an intention to cause harm. The s18 offence is committed when the judges feel that the accused caused grievous bodily harm which had a wider meaning than that described under s20.

5

Property offences

Theft and other related offences

The law covering theft and other related offences is the Theft Act 1968. Theft is a triable either-way offence and the maximum sentence is seven years.

Sections 1-7 of the Theft Act 1968 covers the law of theft with section 1 defining theft. This definition is that a person is guilty of theft if he 'dishonestly appropriates property belonging to another with the intention of permanently depriving the other of it'.

Section 3 of the Theft Act covers the meaning of 'appropriates'. This states:

any assumption by a person of the rights of an owner amounts to be an appropriation, and this includes, where he has come by the property (innocently or not) without stealing it, any later assumption of a right to it by keeping or dealing with it as owner.

A person therefore appropriates property when he assumes the rights of the true owner. One case illustrating this is Pitham and Hehl 1977, where the

Court of Appeal decided that a man who invited the two defendants into his friend's house whilst he was in prison and then sold them some of his furniture, had been assuming the rights of the owner. Not all the rights of the owner need to be appropriated. One case that illustrates this is Anderton and Burnside 1984. In this case, the shopper had removed the price label from a joint of pork and replaced it with a lower price label from another item. He was arrested and appealed on the basis that he had not appropriated property belonging to another, because he had not assumed the rights of the real owner. The appeal was dismissed after the House of Lords decided that they had assumed at least one of the rights of the real owner.

The law on appropriation can be summarised as follows:

- an appropriation will have taken place when just one of the rights of the owner is assumed
- an appropriation can occur even though the owner apparently consents to the appropriation (unknowingly)
- an appropriation may still take place where the defendant appears to have acquired legal ownership of the property
- an appropriation will not, however, take place where the act is not a physical one and is considered too remote

This last point was illustrated in the case of Briggs 2003, where the defendant had handled the purchase of a house called Welwynd Lodge, supposedly for her elderly relatives. She enclosed a letter of authority signed by them, instructing the conveyancers in the sale of the couple's existing property, to send £49,950 of the sale proceeds to the solicitors acting in the sale of Welwynd Lodge and to send the remainder to the relatives bank account. Welwynd Lodge was subsequently registered in the names of the defendant and her father.

The allegation by the prosecution was that the consent of the elderly couple was induced by fraud as they believed that the property was being purchased on their behalf. The defendant was convicted on one count of theft, two counts of forgery, two counts of dishonestly obtaining social security benefits and one count of obtaining property by deception. Briggs was given leave to appeal on the charge of theft only. Although the prosecution had claimed that the defendant had appropriated the credit balance of £49,950 when the conveyancers had transferred the proceeds of the sale to the solicitors involved in selling, the defence argued that a payment transferred in this fashion could not amount to an appropriation within the meaning of s3 of the Theft Act. The Court of Appeal agreed, surprisingly, deciding that the word 'appropriation' required a physical act, not a remote act.

Section 4 (1) of the Theft Act 1968 defines the meaning of 'property' including:

money and all other property, real and personal, including things in action and other intangible property.

Section 4(2) qualifies the meaning by stating that a person cannot steal land, or things forming part of the land, except in specific circumstances, such as the unauthorised disposal of land by a trustee or personal representative, where a person not in possession of the land severs something from it or where a tenant removes something from the land which should have remained attached to the land.

'Things in action'

Things in action are known in civil law as 'choses in action'. They consist of intangible property such as copyrights and patents, shares, debts and insurance policies.

Section 4(3) deals with wild flowers, plants and animals. Section 4(3) states that no offence is committed if a person picks wild mushrooms and flowers, fruit or foliage as long as it is not for commercial purposes. Section 4(4) states that a person will not commit theft if he captures a wild animal which has not been tamed or reduced to captivity.

Section five of the Theft Act 1968 deals with the definition of 'belonging to another'. This section states that:

Property shall be regarded as belonging to any person having possession or control of it, or having in it any proprietary right or interest...

The property can belong to either the owner of it or those who are currently in possession of it or have some right over it.

Section six of the Act defines the meaning of 'permanently depriving the other of property' This covers situations such as the borrowing of property with the intention of returning it. Section seven lays down maximum punishment terms for offences under the Theft Act.

Robbery

Section 8 of the Theft Act 1968 defines robbery as:

A person is guilty of robbery if he steals and immediately before or at the time of doing so and in order to do so, he uses force on any person or seeks to put them in fear of being then and there subject to force.

Section 8(2) of the Act provides for life imprisonment as a maximum sentence. By definition, robbery is aggravated theft so theft must be established first. Several cases highlight the nature of a robbery. In Robinson 1977, the defendant ran a clothing club and was owed money by the victims wife. A fight took place during which £5 fell from the victims pocket. The defendant took this money and further claimed that he was still owed £2.

The Court of Appeal quashed the conviction for robbery as he had a belief that he was entitled to the money and could not be held to have stolen it.

In another case, Hale 1979, the defendant and an accomplice, wearing stocking masks, forced their way into the victim's house, put a hand over her mouth to stop her screaming and then tied her up. Before tying her up, the accomplice had stolen a jewellery box from upstairs. The defendant was convicted of robbery. He appealed stating that because the theft had occurred before the victim was tied up the definition of robbery had not been established.

The Court of Appeal rejected this argument stating that 'the act of appropriation does not suddenly cease. It is a continuous act and it is a matter for the jury to decide whether or not the act of appropriation has finished'.

Burglary

Section 9 of the Theft Act 1968 defines the offence of burglary in two parts:

Under s9(1)(a) the crime is committed where:

- The defendant enters a building or part of one
- As a trespasser
- With the intent to steal, inflict grievous bodily harm, or do unlawful damage to the building or anything inside it.

Under s9(1)(b) the offence is also committed where:

- a person steals or inflicts grievous bodily harm on another
- after he has entered as a trespasser
- or attempts to do either of these things.

Elements of burglary

Entry

The entry must have been effective. This was highlighted by the case of Collins 1973. The defendant who was 19 years old, had seen the girl in question when he worked near her house and after drinking a lot had decided to visit the premises. On seeing a light in her bedroom he fetched a ladder to reach the bedroom. On looking through the window he saw the girl lying on the bed naked and asleep. He walked down the ladder, took off his clothes with the exception of his socks and then climbed the ladder. He alleged that as he was pulling himself into the room the girl awoke. According to him she got up, knelt by the bed, embraced him and appeared to pull him towards it. They then had sexual intercourse.

However, the girl argued that she had awoken at about 3.30am and had seen a vague form with blond hair in the open window. She was unable to say whether the person was outside or inside of the window. She had believed that her boyfriend had come to see her but later, during intercourse she had changed her mind and turned on the light.

Collins was later convicted of burglary. The girl argued that she would not have agreed to the intercourse if she had realised that the man in question was not her boyfriend. The defendant claimed that he would not have entered the room if the girl had not have beckoned him. He was convicted and appealed on the basis that he was not a trespasser.

The Court of Appeal decided that there had to have been an entry into the building. Secondly, the defendant needed to have entered as a trespasser, which was more difficult to decide on. Lastly, he had to have intended, at the time of the entry to commit rape. They stated:

Unless the jury were entirely satisfied that the appellant made an effective and substantial entry into the bedroom without the complainant doing or saying anything to cause him to believe that she was consenting to his entering it, he ought not to be convicted of the offence charged. The point is a narrow one, as narrow maybe as the window sill which is crucial to the case. But this is a criminal charge of gravity and, even though one may suspect that his intention was to commit the offence charged, unless the facts show with clarity that he in fact committed it he ought not to remain convicted.

The fact that there must have been an effective entry has since been disputed, such as in the case Brown 1985, where the Court of Appeal upheld a conviction for burglary even though the defendant argued that his entry was ineffective because a major part of his body was still on the highway. He had been caught whilst leaning through a shop window and sorting out goods.

Therefore, it is the intent and the individual circumstance as well as arguments concerning effective or ineffective entry to a premises.

Trespasser

The courts have held that a person is a trespasser if he enters a premises of another knowing that 'he is entering in excess of the permission given to him, or being reckless to this fact'.

Building

Although there is no definition of a building in the Act, s9(4) states that the word includes an inhabited vehicle and a vessel, even if they are not inhabited at the time of the offence. In Stevens and Gourley 1859, a building was defined as 'a structure of considerable size and intended to be permanent, or at least endure for a considerable time'.

Aggravated burglary

Section 10 of the Theft Act 1968 states that: A person will be guilty of aggravated burglary if he commits any burglary and at the time has with him any firearm or imitation firearm, any weapon of offence or explosive. Section 10(2) gives a wide definition of firearm to include air pistols and any imitation firearm, i.e. something which has the appearance of a firearm whether discharged or not.

Making off without payment and deception offences generally

The Theft Act 1978, s3, covers this area. This section was created to plug a loophole in the Theft Act 1968 where people obtained goods without at that time deceiving the other party but later refusing to pay for them. Section 3 states that:

...a person who, knowing that payment on the spot for any goods supplied or service done is required or expected from him, dishonestly makes off without having paid as required or expected and with intent to avoid payment of the amount shall be guilty of an offence.

This can cover situations such as driving off without paying for petrol or leaving without paying for a meal.

6

Obtaining property by deception

This offence is covered by s 15 of the Theft Act 1968. This section sets out the definition as thus:

A person who by any deception dishonestly obtains property belonging to another, with the intention of permanently depriving the other of it shall on conviction or indictment be liable for imprisonment for a term not exceeding ten years.

Although obtaining property by deception is very similar to the act of theft there are important distinctions. Under s 15, deception has to be practiced so not everyone charged with theft would be guilty of deception. In addition, the maximum sentence is higher.

Definition of deception

There can be no liability under s 15 if the victim has not been deceived. The case of Re London and Globe Finance Corporation 1903 outlined deception as ' to induce a man to believe that a thing is true which is false and which the person practicing the deceit knows or believes to be false.

A person must be involved. There is no liability under s 15 if, for example, a person put foreign coins or tokens of no value in a machine to obtain goods from it. Section 15(4) further clarifies the meaning of deception by stating that it includes deliberate and reckless deception by either words or conduct. Deception can be either express or implied. For example, a person paying for goods by a cheque where he knows that the cheque won't be honoured, provided it can be shown that someone had been deceived.

Obtaining a money transfer by deception

The law covering this is to be found in a new section, s15A, inserted into the Theft Act 1968 by the Theft Amendment Act 1996. In the main, this covers the dishonest receipt of mortgages and other loans by giving false information. Section 15A states:

A person is guilty of an offence if by any deception he dishonestly obtains a money transfer for himself or another.

The maximum punishment laid down in s15A(2) is ten years in prison.

Obtaining pecuniary advantage by deception

Section 16(1) of the 1968 Theft Act covers the above. The Act states:

A person who by any deception dishonestly obtains for himself or another any pecuniary advantage shall on conviction or indictment be liable to imprisonment for a term not exceeding five years.

Under section 16(2)(b) a person unlawfully acquires a monetary advantage if by deception he is permitted to become overdrawn, take out an annuity or insurance policy or to secure an improvement on the terms of any such transaction.

One case that illustrates this is MPC v Charles 1977, where the defendant visited a gaming club and used all his remaining cheques to purchase gambling chips. Each of the cheques was for £30 and covered by a cheque guarantee card so each cheque had to be honoured by the bank involved. The defendant was sued for the money after the cheques were dishonoured and on appeal the conviction was upheld.

Section 16(2) (c) states that a person also commits this offence if, by deception, he is given the opportunity to earn remuneration or greater remuneration in an office or employment. This could occur, for example, if a person lies about qualifications.

Obtaining services by deception

The Theft Act 1978, s1, covers the above. It states:

A person who by any deception dishonestly obtains services from another is guilty of an offence.

S1 (2) states:

It is an obtaining of services where the other is induced to confer a benefit by doing some act, or causing or permitting some act to be done, on the understanding that the benefit has been or will be paid for.

Such benefits could be repairs to the home, car hire and numerous other services provided. S4 states that the maximum punishment is five years imprisonment.

One such case that illustrates obtaining of services by deception is that of Sofroniou 2003. The defendant was convicted of obtaining services by deception, in this case bank loans, credit card facilities and overdraft facilities. He did this by assuming false identities. This case was obscured in that it was not clear, and had not been established, whether the defendant had opened the accounts. Nor was there clear evidence and on what basis the bank would charge for its services. The defendant appealed against his conviction claiming that there was insufficient evidence that he had obtained a service in the first place and that, even if a service had been provided there was insufficient evidence that it had been paid for.

Not surprisingly, the Court of Appeal dismissed his appeal, pointing out the following:

- There was no real or substantial difference in the context of this particular offence between dishonestly obtaining services by credit card or by the dishonest operation of a bank account once opened

- Dishonestly inducing a bank or building society to provide banking or credit card services and the dishonest operation of such an account or the dishonest use of a credit card over a period of time could all come under the ambit of section 1. No distinction should be made between the opening of an account and the later operation of it.
- The words 'on the understanding that the benefit has been or will be paid for' under 1(2), although seemingly subjective, could also cover situations where it was clear from the surrounding circumstances that the service would not be provided free of charge.

Evading liability through deception

The above is covered by s2 of the 1978 Theft Act. Section 2(1)(a) states a person commits an offence if, by deception, he:

Dishonestly secures the remission of the whole or part of any existing liability to make a payment, whether his own liability or another's.

What this means is that by deceiving another party and by acting dishonestly the defendant has managed to get all or part of his or someone else's debt extinguished.

Under s2(1)(b) a person evades liability if:

With intent to make permanent default in whole or in part of any existing liability to make a payment, or with intent to let another do so, he dishonestly induces the creditor or any person claiming payment on behalf of the creditor to wait or forego payment.

Under section 2(1)(c) a person will incur liability if by any deception he:

dishonestly obtains any exemption from or abatement of liability to make a payment.

An example might be where a person deceives the Inland Revenue by misstating his position which leads to a lower tax assessment.

7

Criminal Damage

Criminal damage is covered by the Criminal Damage Act 1971. Section 1(1) of the Act covers the basic offence of criminal damage. S1 (1) states:

A person who without lawful excuse destroys or damages any property belonging to another intending to destroy or damage any such property or being reckless as to whether any such property would be destroyed or damaged shall be guilty of an offence.

If the damage or destruction to property is less than £5,000 it will be summarily tried in the Magistrates Court. If it is above £5,000 the offence comes into the category of a triable either way offence for which the maximum punishment is ten years imprisonment.

When defining 'destroys' the courts have decided that rendering something useless will constitute destruction. Damage is defined as not total destruction but where property is made imperfect or inoperative.

One case illustrating this is Samuels v Stubbs 1972 where a policeman's cap was trampled. The courts decided that the word damage 'is sufficiently wide in its meaning to embrace injury, mischief or harm done to the property'.

Property, under the Criminal Damage Act 1971, is defined as all items of a tangible nature, including money and also animals belonging to another. Although the definition of property is similar to the definition in the Theft Act 1968 there are two distinctions to be made:

- Land cannot be stolen but it can be damaged
- Intangible property, such as patents and copyrights can be stolen but cannot be damaged.

As we have seen, under the basic defence the property has to belong to another. This is not the case for more serious offences. It is not an offence to damage your own property. However, the property has to clearly be one's own. One case that illustrates this is Smith 1974 where the tenant of a ground floor flat damaged floor boards, roofing and other areas of a flat before vacating. He claimed that he had caused the damage whilst in the process of removing some of his own electrical wiring. This had been installed with the landlords permission. He argued that the property belonged to him and he was not liable for criminal damage. Not surprisingly, the Court of Appeal rejected this argument. Property under s10(2) of the Act is treated as belonging to another if that other has custody or control of it, a proprietary right in it, a charge over it or a right under trust. This was the case in the above Smith 1974 where although the landlord had given permission by installing the writing the landlord gained a right or control over the installation.

Defences to Criminal damage

Although all of the usual general defences, described later, are available there is a special defence provided in the act, the defence of lawful excuse. Under s5(2) of the Criminal Damage Act 1971, there are two situations where the defendant can claim this special defence:

1. Where he believes that the owner has consented to the damage or would have consented had he known of the facts.
2. Where he destroys or damages the property of another in order to protect his own or another's property.

If defence number two is claimed then two further points must be proved:

- The defendant must believe that the property in question was in need of immediate protection
- The methods adopted to protect the property were reasonable in the particular circumstances.

Section 5(3) goes on to state ' It is immaterial whether a belief is justified or not if honestly held'.

Several cases have highlighted the defence of lawful excuse. In Jaggard v Dickinson 1981, the defendant was charged with basic criminal damage after breaking into a house belonging to a stranger while under the influence of alcohol. She acted in the belief, mistaken, that the house belonged to her friend. Her friend, so she claimed, would have consented to the breaking of a window if she was aware of the facts. The magistrates convicted her stating that she could not rely on section 5(2)(a) because she was drunk and this was self induced. The Divisional Court overturned the conviction stating:

...Parliament has specifically isolated one subjective element, in the shape of honest belief, and has given it separate treatment and its own special gloss in s5(3). This being so, there is nothing objectionable in giving it special treatment as regards drunkenness, in accordance with the natural meaning of the words.

In Chamberlain v Lindon 1998, the defendant demolished a wall built by a neighbour because he believed that it threatened his right of access. The Divisional Court decided that the defendant had an honest belief that his property was in need of immediate protection, and provided that his belief was honestly held, he was entitled to use the special defence.

Aggravated criminal damage

This offence is committed where a person destroys or damages property, either his own or another's, intending danger to the lives of others. The danger to life must come directly from the damage to the property and not another source. This was illustrated in the case of Steer 1988 where the defendant had quarrelled with his former business partner and had gone to his bungalow in the early hours with a rifle. He woke the occupants by ringing the bell. They looked out to see who it was and he fired one shot in the direction of the occupants plus two further shots, hitting the window and the front door.

The occupants were not injured and it was not suggested that the defendant had fired the gun directly at them.

The defendant was charged under s1(1) and s1(2) of the Criminal Damage Act and also with possessing a firearm with intent to endanger life. He appealed against his conviction under s1(2) arguing that the danger to life in this case was from the rifle shots and not damage to property. The House of Lords agreed and his conviction was quashed.

Arson

A person can be charged with arson under s1(3) of the Criminal Damage Act, in addition to s1(1) and s2(2) if there is damage caused by fire. The maximum sentence for arson is life imprisonment should it be committed in its aggravated form.

8

Parties to a crime

If two or more people commit a crime they are considered to be joint principals. If one party only helps the other with a crime he or she may be known as a secondary offender or accomplice.

The Criminal Law Act 1967 amended the Accessories and Abettors Act 1861. This states that ... *'Whosoever shall aid, abet, counsel and procure* the *commission of any indictable offence shall be liable to be tried, indicted and punished as a principal offender'*.

The principal offender

The perpetrator of the crime is the principal offender. This, as we have seen can be more than one person. The test to decide who is the principal offender is to discover whether his act is the most immediate cause of the *actus reus* or whether he is merely aiding that cause to be effected.

Secondary offenders

There are a number of different types of secondary offender. There are those who aid a perpetrator of a crime by giving help, support or assistance. To abet a perpetrator means to encourage, incite or instigate. Such encouragement would usually be at or near the scene of the crime. To aid or abet implies some sort of active involvement whereas merely being at the scene of the crime doesn't imply involvement.

One case that illustrates aiding and abetting is that of Wilcox v Jeffrey 1951, in which the defendant was the owner of a magazine called Jazz illustrated. He had attended a concert at which a jazz musician had played in direct contravention of an aliens order that prevented him from performing whilst in the United Kingdom. Although there was no direct evidence that the magazine owner had participated in the concert, he had attended and later wrote about the concert which rendered him liable to prosecution.

A person could also aid and abet in cases where he has some responsibility for controlling the other person. One case that illustrated this was Tuck v Robson 1970, where the defendant was a licensee of a public house which the police raided after closing time. Three people were charged with drinking after hours and the publican was charged with aiding and abetting.

To counsel

To counsel parties to a crime is to give them advice and encouragement before the crime is committed. One such case which illustrates this is Calhaem 1985 where the defendant was infatuated with her solicitor. She wished to remove his girlfriend from his life. She hired a private detective to murder the girlfriend. The detective stated that he had no intention of committing the crime but was going along with it and would state that the attempt was unsuccessful. He alleged that he visited the girlfriend's house with this in mind but when she screamed and panicked he killed her.

Despite this contention, the detective was convicted of murder and Calhaem was found guilty of being a secondary offender. She appealed on the grounds that the judge had not directed the jury that her counselling of the contract killer had to be a substantial cause of the killing. The Court of Appeal rejected her appeal agreeing with the trial judge that the word 'counsel' merely meant to 'advise, solicit or something of that sort' and decided that there was no implication in this word that there had to be a causal connection between the counselling and the crime.

To procure

To procure is to 'produce by endeavour'. Lord Widgery stated that: You procure a thing by setting out to see that it happens and taking the appropriate steps to produce that happening.

Procuring may also take place when the principal offender has no knowledge of it. However, it is necessary for some sort of connection to exist between the acts of the secondary offender and the crime committed.

A secondary offender can be found guilty of aiding, abetting, counselling or procuring but only one of these elements needs to be present for him to be found guilty.

Knowledge that a crime is to be committed

In Johnson v Youden and Others 1950, it was stated that before a person can be convicted of aiding and abetting the commission of an offence he must at least know the essential matters which constitute the offence. In Bainbridge 1960, it was decided that the defendant need not know of the precise crime that is to be committed, provided that he possesses not mere suspicion 'but knowledge that a crime of the type in question was intended'.

In the case of Bainbridge, six weeks before the crime took place, Bainbridge used a false name and address to purchase cutting equipment. This was later used by the principal offenders to cut through windows and doors to get at the safe in the bank, which they also cut. Bainbridge was charged as an accessory but tried to claim that he did not know the purpose for which the equipment was being used. Whilst he suspected something illegal he believed that his equipment was going to be used for breaking up stolen goods.

The Court of Appeal held that while it was not enough to show merely that the defendant knew that some sort of illegal activity was going on, it was not necessary to show that he knew the exact time and place of the intended crime. His conviction was upheld.

In addition to the knowledge that the crime was going to be committed the prosecution must also prove that the accomplice had the intention to do the acts that assisted or encouraged the crime. One main case which illustrates this is National Coal Board v Gamble 1959. The Coal Board, through the actions of an employee was found guilty of aiding and abetting because the intention to assist the principal offender was apparent. The employee of the Coal Board operated a weigh bridge and told a driver that his load was nearly four tons overweight. The driver decided to take the risk of driving the load and was issued a ticket to do so by the employee.

The Drivers employers were later found guilty of contravening the Motor Vehicles (Construction and Use) Regulations 1955 and the National Coal Board was also convicted as a secondary offender.

9

Defences in criminal cases

Age and lack of capacity

Criminal law treats the age of the offender in a different way to civil law. There are three categories, which at the moment are under review. Children under 10, between 10 and 14 and over 14.

Below age of ten

The law has the view that a child under ten years of age does not have the capacity to commit a crime. Rightly or wrongly, agree or disagree, this is the law and it is covered by s50 of the Children and Young Persons Act 1933, as amended. If crime is a serious one then the child would be put into care and would not be released back into the community until he or she no longer poses a threat to the wider community.

Between ages of ten and fourteen

The Crime and Disorder Act 1998 outlines the position of this age group of offenders. Children of this age are to be held criminally liable for their actions. Previously, this had not been so but a 1996 case on appeal to the House of Lords concerning a boy of 12, observed by the police on private property holding the handlebars of a motorcycle whilst someone else tampered with it effectively created a new precedent treating those between ten and fourteen as liable.

Children of fourteen and over

A child over 14 years of age is entirely responsible for his or her actions.

Insanity

Insanity, or insane automatism can be a defence against a criminal act. However, a balance has to be struck between the person's insanity and protection of the public. If an offender faces trial, and is considered insane then a plea of not guilty due to insanity will be entered. A range of orders can be imposed on the offender to ensure both his own and the publics safety. Orders arise out of the Criminal Procedures (Insanity and unfitness to Plead) Act 1991, which amended the Criminal procedure (Insanity) Act 1964. These orders are:

- Hospital order without time limit mandatory to murder
- Hospital order with time limit
- Guardianship order
- Supervision and treatment order
- Absolute discharge

Unfitness to plead at trial

If, because of state of mind the defendant is unable to appreciate the significance of the trial then he will be classed as unfit to plead.

Insanity at the time of the crime

In this situation the defendant is considered fit to plead but it is claimed, by either the defence or prosecution that he was insane at the time of the crime.

If the defence of insanity is successful a special verdict is recorded, not guilty by reason of insanity.

Defence of insanity under M'Naughton rules

The rules relating to insanity were laid down after the case of M'Naughton 1843. The accused in this case had tried to kill the Prime Minister at the time, Sir Robert Peel. However, he shot and killed the Prime Minister's private secretary, Edward Drummond instead. M'Naughton was found not guilty by reason of insanity. Rules arose from this case. These state that a jury should be informed that a person is sane and responsible for his crimes unless it can be proved that, at the time of the crime:

He was labouring under such a defect of reason, from disease of the mind, as not to know the nature and quality of the act he was doing, or if he did know it, that he did not know he was doing what was wrong.

The burden of proof is on the defendant to prove insanity. A defect of reason caused by a disease of the mind rendering him incapable of knowing what he was doing, must be proved.

Non-Insane Automatism

If an outside factor causes the defendant to act like an automaton, this may be raised as the defence of automatism. Non-insane automatism results in a complete acquittal if proved.

The essence of the defence is that the defendants actions are completely involuntary. In Hill v Baxter 1958, acts committed after a series of blows to the head were seen as examples of automatism. In another case, Whoolley 1997, the defendant admitted driving very close to a car and a fit of sneezing caused him to crash into this vehicle. The act of sneezing was seen as involuntary and constituted a defence of automatism.

There are limits to the defence and each case is obviously considered on its merit.

Intoxication

If a defendant has voluntarily put himself into a state of intoxication then this will generally not be seen as a defence. However, whilst voluntary intoxication is not a defence in crimes of basic intent such as assault, manslaughter and rape, it might be allowed as a full or partial defence in other crimes such as:

- Aggravated criminal damage with intention of endangering life
- Theft
- GBH or malicious wounding
- Murder, where there is an unlawful killing with malice aforethought.

All these crimes, with the exception of murder, treated as a special case, require some further intention to be established in addition to the basic offence.

Involuntary intoxication

In the case of involuntary intoxication, where the offender was given drink or drugs without his consent or knowledge, a defence might be raised both in cases of specific intent and also basic intent.

In some cases, the courts have considered the side effects of drugs as a defence. In the case of Hardie 1985, the defendant had finished with his girlfriend and he became very upset and took Valium to calm his nerves. Although he had been assured that the tablets would calm him, he fell asleep and during this sleep started a fire in his wardrobe at the flat he was vacating. Although he was initially found guilty the Court of Appeal quashed the conviction on the basis of the effects of the drug.

Mistakes about the law

Although mistakes about the law will not usually provide a defence there are limited circumstances where this can be considered. They are as follows:

- Where the mistake prevents the formation of the *mens rea* of the crime
- Where there is justification or excuse for the defendant's actions
- Where a statute provides for this, as in the Theft Act 1968 and the criminal Damage Act 1971.

Self-defence

Two cases highlight self-defence as a defence of mistake. Williams (Gladstone) 1987, where the defendant mistakenly believed he was observing a mugging taking place and attacked another man. The real situation was that the so-called mugger had grabbed hold of another person because the latter had robbed a woman. The case on appeal was quashed because it was seen as a genuine mistake.

In Beckford 1988, a policeman who shot a man who had been terrorising his family was able to use the defence of mistake because he thought the man was armed.

Necessity

In earlier times this defence was available in specific circumstances such as abortion following rape. However, following the case of Re A (Children) 2000, the defence of necessity has been extended. In this case, an operation was seen as necessary in order to save the life of one of conjoined twins and the operation would lead to the death of the other twin. The Court of Appeal had to decide whether the doctors would be killing this twin unlawfully or whether the action could be justified in the eyes of the law.

The Court of Appeal decided unanimously that the operation would be lawful. It was decided:

- The act was necessary to avoid inevitable and irreparable harm
- No more was planned to be done than was necessary for the purpose to be achieved
- The evil to be inflicted was not disproportionate to the evil to be avoided.

Duress

The defence of duress is available if it is proved that the defendant was forced to commit a criminal act because another is using force or threat against him.

In AG v Whelan 1934, it was stated that the defence of duress exists where the accused is subjected to 'threats of immediate death or serious personal violence so great as to overbear the ordinary powers of human resistance'.

Duress of circumstances

In limited circumstances, the defence of duress of circumstances can be used. The origins of the defence, which is relatively new, began with the case of Willer 1986. The defendant believed that he was going out to meet a fellow radio enthusiast but was directed instead down a narrow alleyway where he and his friends were confronted by a gang of youths. They surrounded his car issuing death threats and tried to drag out the occupants. Willer managed to escape by mounting the pavement and driving through a gap in the road. He then discovered that one of his friends was missing. After he tried to rescue his friend, unsuccessfully, he sought help from the police but, astonishingly, was charged with reckless driving. He was convicted but the conviction was overturned on appeal. The Court of Appeal decided that duress was the necessary defence, as opposed to the defence of necessity.

Marital coercion

This is a very limited defence and only applies to a wife who can prove that she committed an offence other than treason and murder, in the presence of, and under coercion of, her husband.

Public and private defence

A person may use force, as long as it is not unreasonably excessive, in the defence of public and private interests such as:

- To prevent crime or to assist in the lawful arrest of an offender
- Prevent a breach of the peace
- Protect property or prevent trespass
- To protect himself from unlawful violence
- To protect himself from unlawful detention

10

Inchoate Offences

Inchoate offences are incomplete offences. The parties involved might have planned the crime but for various reasons the crime does not happen.

Attempts to commit a crime

The above is covered by the Criminal Attempts Act 1981. s1 (1) states that a person will be guilty of attempt if:

With intent to commit an offence to which this section applies, a person does an act which is more than merely preparatory to the commission of the offence. S4 (1) goes on to state 'the attempt is punishable to the same extent as the substantive offence'.

The *actus reus* of attempt

This will exist where the party 'does an act which is more than merely preparatory to the commission of the offence'. The law makes a clear distinction between acts which are undertaken merely to prepare for the crime in question and acts done after this time which will amount to an attempt.

More than merely preparatory

In the case of Jones 1990, the defendant was unable to accept that his ex-mistress had formed a relationship with another man. The defendant purchased a gun, jumped in the intended victims car. He pointed the loaded gun at the man and stated 'you are not going to like this'. The intended victim grabbed the gun and threw it out of the window and escaped.

The police arrested the defendant who also had another weapon with him, a knife. He claimed that he only intended to kill himself and no one else. He argued that he had three more acts to do before he could be said to be ready to kill anyone: remove the safety catch on the gun, put his finger on the trigger and pull the trigger.

The Court of Appeal agreed that the act of acquiring the gun, loading it and going to the school where the victim was waiting for his daughter was merely preparatory to the commission of the offence. However, once he got into the car and threatened the victim there was sufficient evidence for the consideration of the jury on the charge of attempted murder.

The *mens rea* of attempt

This consists of an intention to bring about the offence. S1(1) states that a person will be guilty of attempt if 'with intent to commit an offence' he does an act which is more than merely preparatory to its commission. Reckless behaviour is not sufficient to create a liability.

Conspiracy to commit a crime

This offence is covered by the Criminal Law Act 1977, as amended by the Criminal Attempts Act 1981 and the Criminal Justice Act 1987.

S1 states that the offence of conspiracy to commit a crime will take place when a party agrees with another or others to pursue a course of conduct which, if carried out, will amount to or involve the commission of an offence, or would do so if something had not happened to make the offence impossible to commit.

The *actus reus* of conspiracy

An agreement with others to pursue a course of conduct which, if carried out, will amount to or involve the commission of an offence.

The *mens rea* of conspiracy

Liability is only incurred if the defendant intends to commit the crime. Intention can be implied from the wording of s1 (1) in which it states that a person must agree with another to pursue a course of conduct.

Incitement

Incitement occurs where a person urges another to commit a crime or tries to influence the mind of another. The courts have decided that incitement can be effected by suggestion, argument, persuasion, or by threats or other pressure.

One case that illustrates incitement is that of Invicta Plastics Ltd v Clare 1976, where a conviction was upheld when an advertisement was placed in a motoring magazine drawing attention to a product which could be used to evade speed traps. This amounted to incitement.

The *mens rea* of incitement

The defendant must be shown to have intended to bring about the criminal result and used persuasion or pressure to achieve this. However, it is not necessary for the offence to have been committed.

11

The Legal System

Criminal cases

Over time, there has been a general increase in recorded crime, with violent crime on the increase. The police are obviously in the front line dealing with crime as a whole. The main police powers are contained within the Police and Criminal Evidence Act (PACE) 1984 with amendments and additions made by the Criminal Justice and Public Order Act 1994 and the Criminal Justice Act 2003. PACE also provides for the codes of practice giving extra details on the procedures for stop and search, detaining, questioning and identifying suspects. These are issued by the Home Secretary.

Police powers

The police have to exercise their powers sensitively and respect the rights of the individual citizen. At the same time they must also have sufficient powers to enable them to do their job.

The law on police powers is mainly contained within the Police and Criminal Evidence Act 1984 and the associated codes of practice contained within section 66 of the act. There are six codes:

- Code A deals with the powers to stop and search
- Code B for the powers to search premises and seize property
- Code C deals with detention, treatment and questioning of subjects
- Code D deals with the rules for identification procedures
- Code E deals with the tape recording of interviews with suspects
- Code F deals with visual recording of interviews

Powers to arrest-serious arrestable offences

Some of the rules only apply to serious arrestable offences. These include murder, treason, manslaughter, rape, hijacking, kidnapping, hostage taking, drug trafficking, firearms offences and causing explosions likely to endanger life or property. Other arrestable offences may only be considered to be serious if they endanger the state or public order or cause death of a person.

Powers to stop and search

The powers of police to stop and search people or vehicles are contained in sections 1-7 of PACE. Section 1 gives police the powers to stop and search people and vehicles in a public place. A public place has a wide meaning and extends to private gardens if the police officer in question has good reason to believe that the suspect does not live at that address. To use this power under PACE the police officer must have reasonable grounds for suspecting that the person is in possession of stolen goods or prohibited articles or goods. These include knives and other weapons which can cause harm or be used in burglary or theft.

Voluntary searches

This is where a person is prepared to submit to a search voluntarily. A voluntary search can only take place where there is power to search anyway. Voluntary searches must be recorded.

Other powers to stop and search

Apart from PACE there are also other Acts of Parliament which give the police the right to stop and search in special circumstances. The Misuse of Drugs Act 1971 allows the police to search for controlled drugs and the Terrorism Act 2000 gives powers to stop and search where there is reasonable suspicion of involvement in terrorism.

Section 60 of the Criminal Justice and Public Order Act 1994 gives the police an additional power of the right to stop and search in anticipation of violence.

Roadside checks

Section 4 of PACE gives police the right to stop and search vehicles if there is a reasonable suspicion that a person who has committed a serious offence is at large in an area.

The power to search premises

In certain circumstances the police have the power to enter and search premises. PACE sets out most of these powers although there are other Acts which provide for this mentioned later.

The police can enter a premises without the occupiers permission if a warrant authorising that search has been obtained from a magistrate. This will normally be issued under section 8 of PACE. The magistrate must be convinced that the police have reasonable grounds for believing that a serious arrestable offence has been committed and that there is material on the premises that will be of substantial value in the investigation of the offence. Search warrants are designed to enable the element of surprise and in the process prevent valuable evidence being removed or destroyed.

A warrant must specify the premises to be searched and, as far as possible, the articles or persons to be sought. One entry only, on one occasion is authorised and entry must be at a reasonable hour unless the police can demonstrate the need to enter at another time. They are also required to identify themselves as police officers and to show the warrant on demand.

The courts have, however, held that the police do not have to follow these requirements precisely if the circumstances of the case make it appropriate to do otherwise.

Powers to enter premises without a search warrant

Police officers may enter and search premises if it is in order to arrest a person named in an arrest warrant, or to arrest someone for an arrestable offence, or to recapture an escaped prisoner. This power is set out in section 17 of PACE. Reason for the entry must be given to anyone in the premises. PACE also gives a police officer the right to enter a premises without a search warrant after an arrest if an officer has grounds to believe that there is evidence on the premises relating to the offence for which the person has just been arrested.

To prevent a breach of the peace

There is a right under common law for police to enter premises if there is a need to deal with or prevent a breach of the peace. This right applies even to private homes as was demonstrated by the case of McLeod v Commissioner of Police for the Metropolis (1994) in which the police had entered domestic premises when there was a violent quarrel taking place.

Searching with the consent of the occupier of the premises

The police may enter and search a premises without a warrant if the occupier of these premises gives them permission to do so. This consent must be given in writing and can be withdrawn.

Unlawful entry and search

If a premises is entered and searched unlawfully, where the police exceed their powers a claim for damages can be made under the tort of trespass.

Powers of arrest

Section 24 of PACE sets out the general powers of arrest, and some of these powers can be exercised by private citizens as well as the police.

Arrestable offences

An arrestable offence is:

1. Any offence for which the sentence is fixed by law. An example may be murder which has a fixed term of life imprisonment.
2. Any offence for which the maximum sentence that could be given to an adult is five years imprisonment.
3. Any other offence which Parliament has specifically made an arrestable offence.

PACE Section 24-Arrests by police and private citizens

This section allows the police or a private citizen to arrest without a warrant:

1. Anyone who is in the act of committing an arrestable offence

2. Anyone whom he has reasonable grounds for suspecting to be committing an arrestable offence
3. Anyone who has committed an arrestable offence
4. Where an arrestable offence has been committed, anyone for whom he has reasonable grounds for suspecting to be guilty of it.

The police also have the right to arrest anyone who is about to commit an arrestable offence, anyone whom he has reasonable grounds for suspecting to be about to commit an arrestable offence or where there are reasonable grounds for suspecting that an arrestable offence has been committed.

PACE Section 25

Police have further powers under section 25 to arrest for any offence where the suspects name and address cannot be discovered or that there are reasonable grounds to believe that the name and address given by the suspect are false.

Section 25 also provides powers of arrest where there are reasonable grounds for believing that arrest is necessary to prevent that person from:

- Causing physical injury to himself or others
- Suffering physical injury (i.e. suicide)
- Causing loss or damage to property
- Committing an offence against public decency
- Causing an unlawful obstruction of the highways

Section 25 also gives the police powers to arrest if the arrest is believed to be necessary to protect a child or other vulnerable person.

Other rights of arrest

The Criminal Justice and Public Order Act 1994 added an extra power of arrest to PACE. This is in section 46A of PACE and gives the police the right to arrest without a warrant anyone who has been released on police bail and fails to attend a police station at an allotted time. The Criminal Justice and Public Order Act also gives police the right to arrest for a variety of new offences in connection with collective or aggravated trespass.

Arrest for breach of the peace

The police have a right to arrest where there has been or is likely to be a breach of the peace. The conditions for arrest for breach of the peace were laid down in *Bibby v Chief Constable of Essex Police (2000)*. These are:

- There must be sufficiently real and present threat to the peace
- The threat must come from the person to be arrested
- The conduct of the person must clearly interfere with the rights of others and its natural consequence must be 'not wholly unreasonable' violence from a third party
- The conduct of the person to be arrested must be unreasonable

The right to search an arrested person

Where a person has been arrested the police have a right to search that person for anything which might be used to help an escape or anything that might be evidence relating to an offence.

Powers to detain suspect

Once a person has been arrested and taken to a police station there are rules setting out time limits as to detention. The limits will vary and are longer depending on the severity of the offence. There are also rules, contained in PACE relating to treatment of people in detention.

The general rules are that the police may detain a person for 24 hours. After this the police can detain a person for a further 12 hours but only with the permission of a senior officer. After 36 hours those detained for an ordinary arrestable offence must be released or charged. For serious offences those detained can be held for a further period but a magistrates order must be obtained and the maximum detention cannot exceed 96 hours. There is a right to representation. There is an exception under terrorism offences which allows for detention of 48 hours and up to another 12 days with the Home Secretary's permission.

Rights of detained people
Detainees must be informed of their rights. These include:
* Someone must/can be informed of the arrest

- Being told that independent legal advice is freely available and being allowed to consult with a solicitor
- Being allowed to consult the code of practice

Police interviews

Detained persons may be interviewed by the police. All interviews carried out at a police station must be tape recorded. Suspects have the right to a solicitor during questioning. If a solicitor is not asked for or is late questioning can commence. If the person is under 17 or is mentally handicapped there must be an 'appropriate adult' present during questioning.

Section 76 of PACE states that a court shall not allow statements which have been obtained through oppression to be used as evidence.

The right to silence

A defendant has the right to remain silent but inferences can be drawn from the silence and used in court. The wording of a caution given to a suspect states:

'You do not have to say anything. But it may harm your defence if you do not mentioned when questioned something which you later rely on in court. Anything you do say may be given in evidence'

Searches, fingerprints and samples

When a person is being held at a police station the police do not have an automatic right to search them. However, a custody officer has a duty to record everything a person has with them and if the custody officer thinks a search is necessary then a non-intimate search can be made. A strip search can only take place if it is necessary to remove an article which a person in detention should not be allowed to keep and there is reasonable suspicion that a person may have concealed an article. There are strict rules governing the nature of a strip search and articles of clothing that can be removed at once and in which places.

The police can take fingerprints and non-intimate body samples without the persons consent. Reasonable force can be used to obtain these if necessary. There are different rules for intimate samples. These are defined in the Criminal Justice and Public Order Act 1994 as:

a) a sample of blood, semen or other tissue, fluid, urine or public hair
b) a dental impression
c) a swab taken from a person's body orifice other than the mouth

These can only be taken by a registered medical practitioner or nurse. Samples can be retained.

Complaints against the police

People who believe that the police have acted unjustly and exceeded their powers can complain and the type of complaint will determine how it is dealt with. Minor complaints are dealt with informally and more serious complaints will be dealt with at a higher level.

The independent police complaints commission

This was set up in 2004 to supervise the handling of complaints against the police and associated staff, such as Community Support Officers. The IPCC sets down standards for the police to follow when dealing with complaints. They also monitor the way complaints are dealt with by local police forces.

The IPCC will also investigate serious issues including any accident involving death or serious injury, allegations of corruption, allegations against senior officers, allegations involving racism and allegations of perverting the course of justice.

Any member of the public can complain and complaints can be made directly to the IPCC or through organisations such as the Citizens Advice Bureau or through the Council for Racial Equality or the Youth Offending Team. It is also possible to complain through a solicitor or an MP. Where the police have committed a crime in the execution of their duties criminal action can be brought against them.

12

Hearing Criminal Cases

As the criminal law is set down by the state, bringing a prosecution for breach of criminal law is seen as the role of the state. The majority of prosecutions are brought by the Crown Prosecution Service which is the agency of the state for criminal prosecutions.

A criminal prosecution can also be brought by an individual or company although this is rare. The following is an outline of the procedure for criminal trials.

Pre-trial hearings

All criminal cases will first go to the magistrates court and, in most cases, will be referred to a higher court unless the offence is minor or the person(s) plead guilty.

Categories of criminal offences

Criminal offences are divided into three main categories as follows:

1. Summary offences. These are the least serious and are always tried in the Magistrates Court. They include nearly all driving offences, common assault and criminal damage of less than £5,000.

2. Triable either-way offences. These are a middle range type offence and can include assault causing actual bodily harm. These cases can be tried either in the Magistrates Court or the Crown Court.

3. Indictable offences. These are more serious crimes such as rape or murder. All such offences must be tried at the Crown Court, the first hearing being at the Magistrates Court.

Bail

One matter to be decided pre-trial is that of bail, whether the defendant should stay in custody while awaiting trial or whether he or she should be released on bail. Being granted bail means that the person is at liberty until the next stage of the case.

The police may release a suspect on bail while they pursue their enquiries. The suspect must return to the police station at a specified date in the future. The police can also grant bail to a defendant who has been charged with an offence. In this case the person is bailed to appear at a Magistrates Court at a later date. The decision on whether to grant bail or not is made by a custody officer under section 38 of PACE. Bail can be refused if the suspects name and address cannot be ascertained or there is doubt as to the validity of information.

The principles as to when bail should be granted are contained within the Bail Act 1976. This is the key Act, starting with the assumption that an accused person should be granted bail, though this right can be limited for certain cases such as terrorism or repeat serious offences. Section 4 of the Bail Act 1976 gives a general right to bail, but this can be withdrawn if the court believes that there are grounds for believing the defendant, if released, would fail to surrender to custody, commit an offence whilst on bail or interfere with witnesses or obstruct the course of justice.

In deciding whether to grant bail the court will consider various factors:

- The nature and seriousness of the offence
- The character of the defendant and community ties
- The record of the defendant
- The strength of evidence against the defendant.

The courts have the powers to impose conditions on the granting of bail. These are similar to those granted to the police, as outlined below.

Bail sureties

The courts or police can require a surety for bail. This is another person who is willing to pay a sum of money if that person doesn't turn up to court. No money is paid until the defendant breaks bail.

If any person granted bail by the police fails to attend the next stage of the case then the police can make an arrest.

Like the courts, the police have powers to impose conditions on bail. These are contained within the Criminal Justice and Public Order Act 1994. These conditions can vary, ranging from surrender of passport to regular reporting at a police station.

If the police are not prepared to grant bail then they must bring the suspect before a magistrates court. The magistrates can then make a decision as to whether the suspect should be released on bail.

Restrictions on bail do exist, such as terrorism cases and situations where there have been repeated serious offences.

Section 19 of the Criminal Justice Act 2003 amended the Bail Act 1976 and placed certain restrictions on bail for adult drug offenders who have tested positive for specific Class A drugs where the offender is either charged with possession or possession with intent to supply a Class A drug or the court is satisfied that there are grounds for believing that misuse of a class A drug contributed to the offence or that the offence was motivated wholly or partly by the intended misuse of a drug and the defendant has refused to participate in an assessment or follow up in relation to the dependency on Class A drugs.

The prosecution in a case can appeal against the granting of bail. This is set out in the Bail (Amendment) Act 1993.

The Crown Prosecution Service

The Crown Prosecution Service (CPS) was established by the Prosecution of Offences Act 1985 and began life in 1986. The head of the CPS is the Director of Public

Prosecutions who must have been a qualified lawyer for 10 years. The DPP is appointed by the Attorney General. Under the DPP are Chief Crown Prosecutors who each head one of 42 areas. Each area is sub-divided into branches, each of which is headed by a Branch Crown prosecutor. Within branches there are lawyers and support staff who are given responsibility for cases.

The functions of the CPS involve all aspects of prosecution as outlined below:

- Deciding on what offences should be charged
- Reviewing all cases given to them by the police to see if there is sufficient evidence to proceed and whether it is in the public interest to do so
- Taking responsibility for the case
- Conducting the prosecution of cases in the Magistrates Court
- Conducting cases in the Crown Court

Once a defendant has been charged with an offence then the police role in the matter is over and the case is handed over to the CPS.

Criminal courts

The two courts which hear criminal cases are the Magistrates Court and the Crown Court. If a defendant in either one of these courts pleads guilty to a charge against them the role of the court is to pass sentence. Where the accused pleads not guilty the role of the court is to try the case and establish whether the defendant is guilty or not guilty. The burden of proof is on the prosecution who must prove the case beyond reasonable doubt. The form of trial is adversarial with prosecution and defence presenting their cases and cross-examining witnesses while the role of the judge is to be a referee, overseeing the trial and ensuring that the law is adhered to. The judge does not investigate the case.

The role of the Magistrates Court

There are about 430 Magistrates Courts in England and Wales. Magistrates Courts are local courts and they will be in almost every town whilst big cities will usually have several. Cases are heard by magistrates, who may be either qualified District Judges or unqualified lay justices. There is a legally qualified clerk attached to each court to provide assistance.

Magistrates Courts have jurisdiction in a variety of matters. They will:

- Try all summary cases
- Try any triable either way offences which it has been decided should be dealt with in the Magistrates Court
- Deal with the first hearings of all indictable offences
- Deal with other matters connected to criminal offences such as issuing warrants for bail and deciding bail applications
- Try cases in the Youth Court where the defendant is aged 10-17

The Magistrates Courts also have some civil jurisdiction including enforcing council tax demands and issuing warrants of entry and investigation to utilities such as gas and electricity, family cases, proceedings concerning the welfare of children under the Children Act 1989.

Summary Trials

Summary trials are the least serious criminal offences. They are further divided into offences on different levels ranging from level one (lowest) to level five (highest). Fines are set in accordance with each level. For level one the fine is maximum £200, level two £500, level three £1,000, level four £2,500 and level five £5,000. These fines arise from the Criminal Justice Act 1991 and are increased periodically to account for inflation. The maximum prison sentence that can be given for summary offences is six months which will shortly be increased to 15 months following the passing of the Criminal Justice Act 2003.

At the start of any summary trial the defendant will be asked whether he or she pleads guilty or not guilty. If a guilty plea is entered the case will be explained to the court and the prosecutor and defence will put their case and the magistrates will decide sentence.

If a not guilty plea is entered, the procedure is rather more complicated as the prosecutor has to provide evidence to the court and prove the case. Witnesses are called. At the end the defence can call for the case to be dismissed on lack of evidence if this is the case. The magistrates will then decide on the case, whether guilty or not guilty.

Triable either-way cases

Plea before venue

Under this procedure the defendant is asked whether he pleads guilty. If the plea is guilty then there is no right to ask to go to a Crown Court although the magistrate may still decide to send him there for sentence.

If the defendant pleads not guilty then the magistrates must carry out 'mode of trial' proceedings to establish where the case will be tried. Under section 19 of the Magistrates Court Act 1980 they must consider the nature and seriousness of the case and decide a course of action. If the case involves complex cases of law it will usually be referred to the Crown Court. It will also be referred to the Crown Court if it is of a particularly serious nature and has, for example, involved organised crime or where the amount involved was particularly high, more than twice the potential fine that magistrates can levy.

In cases, rare cases, where the Attorney General, Solicitor General or Director of Public Prosecutions is the prosecutor, magistrates must abide by the wishes of the prosecutor and send the case to the Crown Court if this is what is wanted.

If magistrates accept jurisdiction, the defendant is informed that he has the right to trial by jury, in the

Crown Court, but may be tried by magistrates if he so wishes. If the magistrates feel that they have insufficient powers to punish they can refer the matter to the Crown Court for sentencing.

Sending cases to the Crown Court

For indictable offences the case is automatically referred by magistrates to the Crown Court. Section 51 of the Crime and Disorder Act 1988 dictates this. For triable either-way offences, magistrates will hold a plea before venue and, if the plea is not guilty, a mode of trial hearing. The decision to try the case in the Magistrates Court or the Crown Court is taken at this point.

Committal proceedings

Magistrates can commit a defendant charged with a triable either-way offence for sentence in the Crown Court.

Role of the court clerk

Every bench of magistrates is assisted by a clerk who is also a legal advisor. The senior clerk in each court has to be a barrister or solicitor of at least five years standing. The role of the clerk is to guide the magistrates on questions of law, practice and procedure.

Youth courts

Youth offenders aged between 10-17 are dealt with in the Youth court which is a branch of the Magistrates court.

Children under the age of 10 cannot be charged with a criminal offence. There are some exceptional cases where the case can be tried in the Crown Court if the charge is one of manslaughter or murder, rape or causing death by dangerous driving. In addition, it is possible to send a person over 14 to the Crown Court if the charge is sufficiently serious.

Appeals from the Magistrates Court

The system of appeal routes from the magistrate's court will depend on whether the appeal is on a point of law or for other reasons. The two appeal routes are the Crown Court or the Queens Bench Divisional Court.

The normal route of appeal is the Crown Court and can only be used by the defence. If the defendant has pleaded guilty then the appeal can only be against sentence. If the plea was not guilty then the appeal can be against conviction or sentence. In both cases the defendant has the automatic right to appeal.

Further appeal to the House of Lords

From the decision of the Queens Bench Court there is a possibility of a further appeal to the House of Lords. This can only be made if:

1. The Divisional Court certifies that a point of law of general public importance is involved.
2. The Divisional Court or the House of Lords gives leave to appeal because the point is one which ought to be considered by the House of Lords.

The Crown Court

The Courts Act 1971 set up the Crown Court to deal with all cases that were not tried at the Magistrates Court. The Crown Court sits in 90 different centres throughout England and Wales. There are three kinds of centre:

1. First tier-these exist in main centres throughout the country. At each court there is a High court and a Crown Court. The Crown Court is staffed by High Court Judges as well as Circuit Judges and Recorders. The court can deal with all categories of crime triable on indictment.
2. Second tier-this is a Crown Court only, but High Court judges can sit there on a regular basis to hear cases, as well as Circuit Judges and Recorders.
3. Third tier-this is staffed by Circuit judges and Recorders. The most serious cases are not usually tried here.

Preliminary matters in the Crown Court

The indictment

The indictment is a document which formally sets out charges against a defendant.

Disclosure by prosecution and defence

The Criminal Procedure and Investigations Act 1996 places a duty on both sides to make certain points of the case known to each other. The 1996 Act also imposes a duty on the defence in cases which are to be tried on indictment. After the prosecutors initial disclosure, the defence must give a written statement to the prosecution setting out:

1. the nature of the accused persons defence
2. the matters on which he takes issue with the prosecution and why he intends to take issue
3. any point of law which he wishes to take, and the case authority on which he will rely.

Details of alibis and witnesses he intends to call to support the alibi. This information gives the prosecution time to carry out police checks on the witnesses.

A preliminary hearing called a 'plea and directions' hearing is held after a case has been forwarded to a Crown Court, normally within four weeks if the defendant is being held in custody and six weeks if not. The purpose of this hearing is to discover whether the plea is guilty or not guilty. All charges are read out in open court and the defendant will plead one way or the other. This is called the 'arraignment'. If the defendant pleads guilty the judge will sentence the defendant immediately, if possible. Where a defendant pleads not guilty the judge will require the defence and prosecution to identify the key issues of fact and law that are involved in the case. He will then give directions that are necessary for the organisation of the trial.

The trial

A defendant appearing at the Crown Court will usually be represented by a barrister and sometimes a solicitor.

Defendants can represent themselves and can, in most cases, cross-examine witnesses although there are some cases where this cannot happen, such as sexual offences.

The order of events at a trial will depend on whether the defendant pleads guilty or not guilty. If the plea is not guilty the following will happen:

- The jury is sworn in to try the case
- The prosecution will make an opening speech outlining the case to the jury
- The prosecution witnesses give evidence and can be cross examined by the defence-other evidence can be produced
- At the end of the prosecutions presentation the defence can state that there is no case to go to the jury: if the judge decides that this is so then he will direct the jury to acquit the defendant
- The defence may make an opening speech provided that they intend calling evidence other than the defendant
- The defence witnesses give evidence and are cross examined by the prosecution
- The prosecutor makes a closing speech pointing out the strengths of the case to the jury
- The defence makes a closing speech pointing out the weaknesses of the case
- The judge sums up the case to the jury and directs them on any law relevant to the case
- The jury retire to consider their verdict
- The jury returns and gives their verdict

- If the verdict is guilty the judge then sentences the accused, if not guilty the defendant is discharged.

It is normal, once acquitted, that the defendant cannot be re-tried. However, Under the Criminal Justice Act 2003 the double jeopardy rule was removed for serious cases if new and compelling evidence comes to light.

Appeals in criminal cases

The defendant can appeal against conviction to the Court of Appeal (Criminal Division). The appeal must be lodged verbally at the court or within 14 days of the sentence in writing. A notice of appeal must be lodged with the Court of Appeal within 28 days.

The Criminal Appeal Act 1995 states that the Court of Appeal:

a) shall allow an appeal against conviction if they think that the conviction is unsafe; and
b) shall dismiss such an appeal in any other case.

The Court of Appeal can allow an appeal and quash the conviction, vary the sentence or overturn the appeal. A re-trial can also be ordered with a new jury.

The prosecution also has limited rights of appeal. In the case of jury tampering an appeal against a not guilty finding is allowed. In addition, under s 36 of the Criminal Justice Act 1972 the Attorney General can refer a point of law to the Court of Appeal. The decision does not affect the acquittal but can influence future law.

Under s36 of the Criminal Justice Act 1988 the Attorney general can apply for leave to refer what is considered to be an unduly lenient sentence to the Court of Appeal for re-sentencing.

Appeals to the House of Lords

Both prosecution and defence may appeal from the Court of Appeal to the House of Lords. However, it is necessary to get the case certified as involving a point of law of general public importance, either from the Court of appeal or the House of Lords.

References to the European Court of Justice

In a case where a point of European law is involved it is possible for any court to make reference to the European Court of Justice under Article 177 of the Treaty of Rome.

Sentencing

Judges and magistrates have a fairly wide discretion when it comes to passing sentence on a guilty party, although they are subject to certain restrictions. Magistrates can only impose a maximum of six months imprisonment for one offence and twelve months for two. The Criminal Justice Act 2003 provides powers to increase the sentence for one offence to 12 months and two or more offences 15 months.

Judges in the Crown Court can impose up to life imprisonment for some crimes and there is no maximum figure for fines.

There are certain other restrictions placed on the Magistrates and Crown Courts by Parliament. The maximum sentence to be handed out varies depending on the crime and Parliament determines the length of sentences.

Murder carries a mandatory life sentence, whereas the judge can work within the parameters of maximum of life for other crimes such as rape and manslaughter.

When judges or magistrates pass sentence they will look at what they are trying to achieve when sentencing. Section 142 of the Criminal Justice Act 2003 sets out the purpose of sentencing for those aged 18 and over. This states that the court must have regard to:

- the punishment of offenders
- the reduction of crime
- the reform and rehabilitation of offenders
- the protection of the public
- the making of reparation by offenders to persons affected by their offences

Courts have several different types of sentences available to them. There are four main categories: custodial sentences, community sentences, fines and discharges.

Custodial sentences

This is imprisonment and is the most serious sentence that a court can pass. Prison can range from a weekend to life. Custodial sentences include:

- mandatory and discretionary life sentences
- fixed term sentences
- short term sentences
- intermittent custody
- suspended sentences

Community sentences

Prior to the Criminal Justice Act 2003, the courts had individual community sentences that they could impose on an offender. The Act created one community order under which the courts can combine any requirements that they think are necessary. These requirements include all the previous existing community sentences which become available as 'requirements' or sentences required to rehabilitate the offender, and can be attached to the sentence. The sentence is available for offenders of 16 or over. The full list of 'requirements' is set out in s 177 of the Criminal Justice Act 2003 which states:

'177 (1) Where a person aged 16 or over is convicted of an offence, the court by or before which he is convicted may make an order imposing on him any one or more of the following requirements:

a) an unpaid work requirement
b) an activity requirement
c) a programme requirement
d) a prohibited activity requirement
e) a curfew requirement
f) an exclusion requirement
g) a residence requirement
h) a mental health treatment requirement

i) a drug rehabilitation requirement
j) an alcohol treatment requirement
k) a supervision requirement
l) in the case where an offender is under 25, an attendance centre requirement.

Fines

The maximum fine in a Magistrates court is £5,000. The magistrates can impose a fine of up to £20,000 on businesses which have committed offences under various regulatory legislation such as health and safety at work.

Discharges

A discharge can be conditional or absolute. Conditional discharge means that the discharge is on condition that no further offence is committed in a set period up to three years. An absolute discharge means that no penalty has been imposed.

Other powers available to the courts

Courts can order compensation to a victim of crime. In the Magistrates court the maximum compensation is £5,000. If the defendant still has the property that he took from the victim then the court can order that it be returned. This is called a restitution order.

A court can order that a person be deprived of property that he has used to commit the offence. There is special power to order forfeiture in drug related cases. The

Proceeds of Crime Act 1995 also gives the courts powers to take from criminals all profits from crime for up to six years before conviction.

Young offenders

As with adult offenders the courts have powers to order custodial sentences, fines and discharges but there are a range of different sentences available and also restrictions on what the courts can order. As far as community sentences are concerned, young offenders aged 16 or over can be given the same sentences as adults. They cannot be used for offenders under the age of 16. However, Curfew Orders can be used for those over 10 years of age. There are a number of other orders aimed at young offenders:

Attendance centre orders

This type of order is only for those under 25 and is available for all young offenders from 10 years onwards. It involves attendance at a special centre for two or three hours a week up to a maximum of 36 hours for 16-24 year olds and 24 hours for 10-15 year olds. The minimum number of hours is usually 12 but can be less for offenders under 14. The centres are run by the probation services and are usually on a Saturday afternoons. An attendance centre order cannot be made if an offender has served a period of detention previously.

Supervision orders

Section 69 of the Crime and Disorder Act 1998 created a new community order called an Action Plan order. The courts can impose this on offenders under the age of 18. The order places the offender under supervision and also sets out requirements the offender has to comply with in respect to his actions and whereabouts during a period of three months. The requirements can be any one of the following:

- To participate in set activities
- To present himself to a specified person at set times and places
- To attend at an attendance centre
- To stay away from certain places
- To comply with arrangements for his education
- To make reparation

Fines for young offenders

The maximum amount of the fine varies with the age of the offender. 10-13 year olds can only be fined a maximum of £250, 14-17 year olds £1,000. Those over 18 are subject to adult rules.

Reparation orders

A Reparation Order may be imposed on offenders under the age of 18. This order cannot be made in combination with a custodial sentence. Community Service Order, a combination order, a supervision order or an Action Plan Order.

An order will require the defendant to make reparation as defined in the order:

- To a person or persons who were victims of the offence or were otherwise affected by it, or
- To the community at large

The order is for a maximum of 24 hours work and the order must be completed under supervision within three months of its imposition. An order for direct reparation to a person can only be made with that persons consent.

Discharges

These may be used for an offender of any age and are most commonly used for young first time offenders who have committed minor crimes. The courts cannot conditionally discharge an offender where a child or young offender has been warned within the previous two years, unless there are exceptional circumstances. Also, the courts cannot conditionally discharge an offender where the offender is in breach of an anti-social behaviour order or where the offender is in breach of a sex offender order.

Reprimands and warnings

These are methods with which the police can deal with young offenders without bringing them to court. There is a limit to the number of times and occasions that an offender can be cautioned.

Responsibility of parents

Parents can be bound over to keep their child under control for a set period of time up to one year. The parents must agree to this. If the child then commits an offence within this period the parents must pay a sum up to £1,000 maximum.

Where an offender under 16 is fined or ordered to pay compensation, the court must order the parents to pay. The financial situation of the parents is taken into account when assessing the amount.

Parenting orders

Parenting orders are intended to offer training and support to parents to help change their children's offending behaviour. Under a parenting order a parent can be required to attend counselling or guidance sessions for up to three months on a basis of a maximum once per week.

In addition, the parent may be required to comply with conditions imposed by the court. A court may make a parenting order where:

- The court makes a Child safety Order
- The court makes an anti-social behaviour order or sex offender order in respect of the child
- A child or young person is convicted of an offence
- A parent is convicted of an offence related to truancy under the Education Act 1996.

Offenders who are mentally ill

The law recognises, as far as it possibly can, that mentally ill offenders should receive treatment as opposed to punishment. Courts have a wide range of powers available to them when dealing with such offenders. The main extra powers available to courts are to give the offender a community sentence with a requirement that he or she attends for treatment, make a hospital order or to make a restriction order under the Mental Health Act 1983 section 41.

Under the same section, offenders with severe mental health problems can be sent to high security hospitals such as Broadmoor. Such an order can only be made by the Crown Court.

Anti-social behaviour orders

Known as ASBO's these are civil orders. They are imposed on a person who has behaved in an anti-social way. The type of behaviour termed anti-social is very wide and can include drunkenness, drug taking or causing prolonged and excessive nuisance to neighbours or the wider community.

 Under an ASBO a person can be ordered not to repeat a certain anti-social behaviour or not to go to a certain place. In short it has the effect of an injunction.

Index